35

STUDY GUIDE

Norman England, c1066–c1100

AQA - GCSE

app
available

Published by Clever Lili Limited.

contact@cleverlili.com

First published 2020

ISBN 978-1-913887-34-6

Cover by: Bayeux Tapestry on Wikimedia Commons

Icons by: flaticon and freepik

Contributors: Jenny Mellors, Marcus Pailing, Alex Price

Edited by Paul Connolly and Rebecca Parsley

Design by Evgeni Veskov and Will Fox

DISCOVER MORE OF OUR GCSE HISTORY STUDY GUIDES

GCSEHistory.com and Clever Lili

AQA - GCSE

STUDY GUIDE

Britain: Health and the People, c1000 to the Present Day

GCSEHistory.com

25

AQA - GCSE

STUDY GUIDE

Elizabethan England, c1568–1603

GCSEHistory.com

26

AQA - GCSE

STUDY GUIDE

Conflict and Tension between East and West, 1945–1972

GCSEHistory.com

27

AQA - GCSE

STUDY GUIDE

Germany, 1890–1945: Democracy and Dictatorship

GCSEHistory.com

28

AQA - GCSE

STUDY GUIDE

America, 1920–1973: Opportunity and Inequality

GCSEHistory.com

29

AQA - GCSE

STUDY GUIDE

Britain: Power and the People, c1170 to the Present Day

GCSEHistory.com

30

AQA - GCSE

STUDY GUIDE

Conflict and Tension: The First World War, 1894–1918

GCSEHistory.com

36

AQA - GCSE

STUDY GUIDE

Russia, 1894–1945: Tsardom and Communism

GCSEHistory.com

43

AQA - GCSE

STUDY GUIDE

America, 1840–1895: Expansion and Consolidation

GCSEHistory.com

38

AQA - GCSE

STUDY GUIDE

Conflict and Tension: The Inter-War Years, 1918–1939

GCSEHistory.com

41

AQA - GCSE

STUDY GUIDE

Britain: Migration, Empires and the People, c790 to the Present Day

GCSEHistory.com

44

AQA - GCSE

STUDY GUIDE

Conflict and Tension in Asia, 1950–1975

GCSEHistory.com

45

THE GUIDES ARE EVEN BETTER WITH OUR GCSE/IGCSE HISTORY WEBSITE APP AND MOBILE APP

GCSE History is a text and voice web and mobile app that allows you to easily revise for your GCSE/IGCSE exams wherever you are - it's like having your own personal GCSE history tutor. Whether you're at home or on the bus, GCSE History provides you with thousands of convenient bite-sized facts to help you pass your exams with flying colours. We cover all topics - with more than 120,000 questions - across the Edexcel, AQA and CIE exam boards.

GCSEHistory.com

Contents

In this study guide, you will see a series of icons, highlighted words and page references. The key below will help you quickly establish what these mean and where to go for more information.

Icons

WHAT questions cover the key events and themes.

WHO questions cover the key people involved.

WHEN questions cover the timings of key events.

WHERE questions cover the locations of key moments.

WHY questions cover the reasons behind key events.

HOW questions take a closer look at the way in which events, situations and trends occur.

IMPORTANCE questions take a closer look at the significance of events, situations, and recurrent trends and themes.

DECISIONS questions take a closer look at choices made at events and situations during this era.

Highlighted words

Abdicate - occasionally, you will see certain words highlighted within an answer. This means that, if you need it, you'll find an explanation of the word or phrase in the glossary which starts on **page 77**.

Page references

Tudor *(p.7)* - occasionally, a certain subject within an answer is covered in more depth on a different page. If you'd like to learn more about it, you can go directly to the page indicated.

Norman England, 1066-c.1100 is a British depth study that investigates how England changed and developed following the Norman Conquest in 1066. The course focuses on the period from 1066 to the years around the accession of Henry I in 1100. You will focus on crucial events during this period, and study the different social, cultural, political, economic and religious changes that occurred. You will also investigate a specific historical site in detail to examine the relationship between the site and events during this time period.

Purpose

This study will help you to understand the reasons for the Norman Conquest in 1066, and the way in which England was ruled by William I and his immediate successors. You will investigate themes such as power, law and order, government, religion, and economy and society. This course will enable you to develop the historical skills of causation, consequence, importance, continuity, and change. You will also learn to critically evaluate historical interpretations.

Enquiries

Norman England, 1066-c.1100 is split into four key enquiries: Conquest and control, Life under the Normans, The Normans and the Church, and the historic environment.

- Enquiry 1 looks at the succession crisis following the death of Edward the Confessor in 1066, and the subsequent battles for the throne. You will also study how William I consolidated his rule in the years after the Battle of Hastings, including his methods of dealing with rebellions against his rule.

- Enquiry 2 looks at how the Normans used the Feudal System to govern England. You will also learn what life was like for ordinary people in towns and villages under Norman rule.

- Enquiry 3 looks at the relationship between the Normans and the Church. You will learn how the Normans reformed the Church and monasteries, and how the relationship of the king with the pope in Rome changed over time.

- Enquiry 4 looks at the historic environment. The site chosen changes each year and you have to investigate how the site and historical developments in this period link together.

Key Individuals

Some of the key individuals studied on this course include:

- Edward the Confessor.
- William I (William the Conqueror).
- Harold Godwinson.
- Harald Hardrada.
- Edgar Aetheling.
- William II (William Rufus).
- Henry I.
- Lanfranc, Archbishop of Canterbury.
- Anselm, Archbishop of Canterbury.

Key Events

Some of the key events you will study on this course include:

- The Battle of Stamford Bridge.
- The Battle of Hastings.
- The Saxon rebellions of 1067-1071.
- The Harrying of the North, 1069-70.
- The Earls' Revolt of 1075.
- The creation of the Domesday Survey.
- The continuation of the Norman dynasty after the death of William I.

Assessment

Norman England, 1066-c.1100 forms part of paper 2 which you have a total of two hours to complete. You should spend one hour on this section of the paper. There will be four exam questions which will assess what you have learnt on the Norman England, 1066-c.1100 course.

Question 1 is worth 8 marks. This question requires you to examine an interpretation, and assesses your ability to analyse and evaluate how convincing the interpretation is, using your contextual knowledge to challenge or corroborate what is being said.

Question 2 is worth 8 marks. This question will require you to explain the importance of a different theme or event by using your contextual knowledge and looking at the consequences or impact of the event.

Question 3 is worth 8 marks. This question will require you to show your knowledge and understanding of the key features and characteristics of the course. You will have the opportunity to show your ability to explain and analyse historical events using second order concepts such as causation, consequence, change, continuity, similarity and difference.

Question 4 is worth 16 marks, and focuses on the Historic Environment site that you will have studied. You will be assessed on similar skills to those in Question 3, but you will also be required to make a judgement in an extended response to the set question.

Revision! A dreaded word. Everyone knows it's coming, everyone knows how much it helps with your exam performance, and everyone struggles to get started! We know you want to do the best you can in your GCSEs, but schools aren't always clear on the best way to revise. This can leave students wondering:

✔ How should I plan my revision time?

✔ How can I beat procrastination?

✔ What methods should I use? Flash cards? Re-reading my notes? Highlighting?

Luckily, you no longer need to guess at the answers. Education researchers have looked at all the available revision studies, and the jury is in. They've come up with some key pointers on the best ways to revise, as well as some thoughts on popular revision methods that aren't so helpful. The next few pages will help you understand what we know about the best revision methods.

 ## How can I beat procrastination?

This is an age-old question, and it applies to adults as well! Have a look at our top three tips below.

◎ Reward yourself

When we think a task we have to do is going to be boring, hard or uncomfortable, we often put if off and do something more 'fun' instead. But we often don't really enjoy the 'fun' activity because we feel guilty about avoiding what we should be doing. Instead, get your work done and promise yourself a reward after you complete it. Whatever treat you choose will seem all the sweeter, and you'll feel proud for doing something you found difficult. Just do it!

◎ Just do it!

We tend to procrastinate when we think the task we have to do is going to be difficult or dull. The funny thing is, the most uncomfortable part is usually making ourselves sit down and start it in the first place. Once you begin, it's usually not nearly as bad as you anticipated.

◎ Pomodoro technique

The pomodoro technique helps you trick your brain by telling it you only have to focus for a short time. Set a timer for 20 minutes and focus that whole period on your revision. Turn off your phone, clear your desk, and work. At the end of the 20 minutes, you get to take a break for five. Then, do another 20 minutes. You'll usually find your rhythm and it becomes easier to carry on because it's only for a short, defined chunk of time.

 ## Spaced practice

We tend to arrange our revision into big blocks. For example, you might tell yourself: "This week I'll do all my revision for the Cold War, then next week I'll do the Medicine Through Time unit."

This is called **massed practice**, because all revision for a single topic is done as one big mass.

But there's a better way! Try **spaced practice** instead. Instead of putting all revision sessions for one topic into a single block, space them out. See the example below for how it works.

This means planning ahead, rather than leaving revision to the last minute - but the evidence strongly suggests it's worth it. You'll remember much more from your revision if you use **spaced practice** rather than organising it into big blocks. Whichever method you choose, though, remember to reward yourself with breaks.

Spaced practice (more effective):

week 1	week 2	week 3	week 4
Topic 1	Topic 1	Topic 1	Topic 1
Topic 2	Topic 2	Topic 2	Topic 2
Topic 3	Topic 3	Topic 3	Topic 3
Topic 4	Topic 4	Topic 4	Topic 4

Massed practice (less effective)

week 1	week 2	week 3	week 4
Topic 1	Topic 2	Topic 3	Topic 4

What methods should I use to revise?

Self-testing/flash cards	Self explanation/mind-mapping
	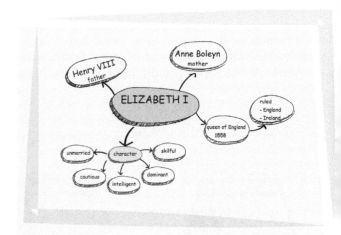

The research shows a clear winner for revision methods - **self-testing**. A good way to do this is with **flash cards.** Flash cards are really useful for helping you recall short – but important – pieces of information, like names and dates.

Side A - question

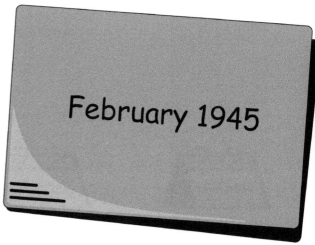

Side B - answer

Write questions on one side of the cards, and the answers on the back. This makes answering the questions and then testing yourself easy. Put all the cards you get right in a pile to one side, and only repeat the test with the ones you got wrong - this will force you to work on your weaker areas.

pile with right answers

pile with wrong answers

As this book has a quiz question structure itself, you can use it for this technique.

Another good revision method is **self-explanation**. This is where you explain how and why one piece of information from your course linked with another piece.

This can be done with **mind-maps**, where you draw the links and then write explanations for how they connect. For example, President Truman is connected with anti-communism because of the Truman Doctrine.

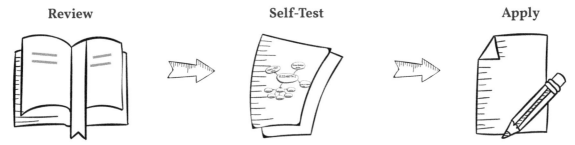

Review

Start by highlighting or re-reading to create your flashcards for self-testing.

Self-Test

Test yourself with flash cards. Make mind maps to explain the concepts.

Apply

Apply your knowledge on practice exam questions.

Which revision techniques should I be cautious about?

Highlighting and **re-reading** are not necessarily bad strategies - but the research does say they're less effective than flash cards and mind-maps.

Highlighting

Re-reading

If you do use these methods, make sure they are **the first step to creating flash cards**. Really engage with the material as you go, rather than switching to autopilot.

TIMELINE

Edward the Confessor became King of England — **1042**

1045 — Edward the Confessor married Edith of Wessex

Earl Godwin rebelled and was forced into exile — **1050**

1051 — Edward the Confessor named William of Normandy as his heir

Harold Godwinson became Earl of Wessex — **1053**

1055 — Tostig Godwinson became Earl of Northumbria

Harold and Tostig Godwinson attacked Gruffudd ap Llywelyn — **1062**

1064 — Harold Godwinson in Normandy

Rebellion against Tostig Godwinson in Northumbria — **1065**

1066 — *January* - Edward the Confessor died. Harold Godwinson became King of England

20th September - The Battle of Gate Fulford *(p.25)*

25th September - The Battle of Stamford Bridge *(p.26)*

14th October - The Battle of Hastings *(p.28)*

25th December - William of Normandy was crowned King William I *(p.31)*

Rebellions against William I on the Welsh borders, in Kent, and in Northumbria — **1067**

1068 — Rebellion against William I in the south-west. In the north, Edwin and Morcar rebelled against Norman rule *(p.36)*

Edgar Aetheling rebelled against William I — **1069**

1069-70 - The Harrying of the North *(p.39)*

1070 — *1070-71* - The East Anglian Revolt *(p.40)*

1070 - Lanfranc was appointed as Archbishop of Canterbury

Thomas, Archbishop of York, accepted the primacy of Canterbury — **1072**

1075 — The Earls' Revolt *(p.41)*

The Domesday Survey *(p.64)* — **1085**

1087 — William Rufus became King of England. Robert Curthose became Duke of Normandy

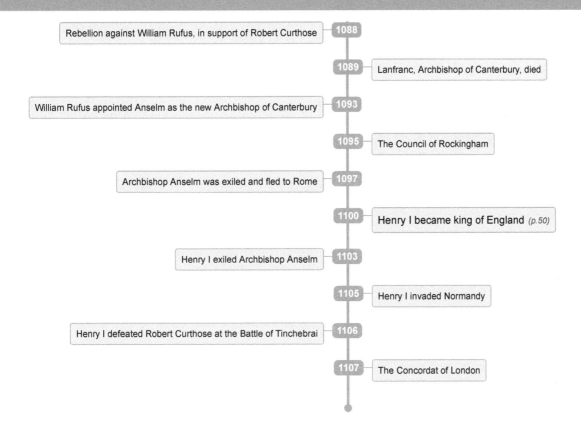

Rebellion against William Rufus, in support of Robert Curthose — **1088**

1089 — Lanfranc, Archbishop of Canterbury, died

William Rufus appointed Anselm as the new Archbishop of Canterbury — **1093**

1095 — The Council of Rockingham

Archbishop Anselm was exiled and fled to Rome — **1097**

1100 — Henry I became king of England *(p.50)*

Henry I exiled Archbishop Anselm — **1103**

1105 — Henry I invaded Normandy

Henry I defeated Robert Curthose at the Battle of Tinchebrai — **1106**

1107 — The Concordat of London

THE POWER OF THE SAXON KINGS
The role and powers of the king in Saxon England.

 What did the king do in Anglo-Saxon society?

The king was the most important person in Anglo-Saxon society and fulfilled a number of roles.

 Who was the king of Anglo-Saxon England in 1060?

In 1060 the king of England was Edward the Confessor. He ruled from 1042 to 1066.

 Could the king make laws in Anglo-Saxon England?

Kings created 'Codes of Law' and distributed them through the country. The king was responsible for the 'King's Peace' and enforcing the laws overall, while the local lords and communities made sure that they were followed.

 How did the king control money in Anglo-Saxon England?

The king controlled the production of silver coins that were used as currency. Counterfeiting coins was a serious crime.

 How did the Anglo-Saxon king control land?

The king owned large portions of land and could grant it or take it away. Those who received it had to pay taxes and serve in the army.

 How much control did the Anglo-Saxon kings have over the army?

The king could raise an army. Landowners had to bring and equip soldiers, or risk being fined or losing their land.

 How did the king collect taxes in Anglo-Saxon England?

The king raised taxes through a national taxation system. He decided when taxes should be paid, and landowners had to pay or risk losing their land.

EDWARD THE CONFESSOR
The life and reign of Edward the Confessor.

Who was Edward the Confessor?

Anglo-Saxon King Edward the Confessor ruled England from 1042 to 1066. When he died there was disagreement about who should succeed him to the throne.

How strong was Edward the Confessor?

Edward the Confessor generally managed to keep control, but problems developed during his reign.

- ☑ His earls and thegns were a powerful military force, and he relied on them to protect England from attack.
- ☑ He was a respected law-maker, who made decisions that kept the King's Peace and prevented in-fighting.
- ☑ He was very religious. Edward built Westminster Abbey, and reflected the Anglo-Saxon view of the king as an agent of God.
- ☑ However, he was not a warrior king, and did not win battles that allowed him to hand out land and money to his earls.

☑ Under Edward, Earl Godwin of Wessex and his family grew so strong that they had more military power than Edward.

 ## What was Edward the Confessor's relationship with Normandy?

Although the Normans were a threat to England, Edward the Confessor had a strong relationship with them.

☑ His mother Emma, was a Norman.

☑ He went into exile in Normandy from 1016 to 1041, when the Vikings took over England.

☑ When he became king in 1042, Edward brought Norman advisers and supporters back to England with him.

☑ The Normans claimed that Edward promised the throne to William, duke of Normandy in return for his support against Earl Godwin.

 ## What happened when Edward the Confessor died?

When Edward the Confessor died in January 1066, the Witan crowned Harold Godwinson as king.

 ## Why did Edward the Confessor's death lead to a succession crisis?

Because Edward the Confessor died without an heir, it was not clear who should succeed him. The problem was that there was no definite way of choosing a successor.

☑ It helped to be a relative of the previous king, but it was not a guarantee.

☑ The Saxons thought that the previous king's dying words (novissima verba) were more important than any previous promises.

☑ However, the Normans considered that earlier promises were stronger, and could not be overturned.

☑ Ultimately, the Witan had to approve the next king, so it was possible for any potential king to influence their decision.

DID YOU KNOW?

Two facts about Edward the Confessor.

✔ Edward the Confessor built Westminster Abbey in London, although it was rebuilt in the 13th century.

✔ Edward was made a saint, so he became Saint Edward the Confessor.

EARL GODWIN

The Godwin family - its power and relationship with Edward the Confessor.

 ## Who was Earl Godwin?

Godwin was a powerful Anglo-Saxon who was made Earl of Wessex in 1018 by King Cnut. Until his death in 1053 he built up the House of Godwin to become a powerful family. His power in England rivalled even that of Edward the Confessor.

 ## Why was Earl Godwin so powerful?

There were a number of reasons why Godwin was able to become so powerful.

☑ King Edward allowed him to build (p. 72) up his power, even though it meant that he could become a threat.

☑ He held extensive lands and was therefore very rich.

☑ He had a large family and a lot of sons, which meant that he had a lot of influential people protecting his interests.

- His family made good political marriages, which meant that he had family connections and ties of loyalty with Edward the Confessor, as well as with other earls and thegns.
- In 1045, Edward married Godwin's daughter, Edith, making Godwin the king's father-in-law.
- Edward was not a strong king, and relied on Godwin to help him keep control. This gave Godwin a lot of influence.

Why did Edward the Confessor allow Earl Godwin to build up his power?

There were a number of reasons why Edward the Confessor allowed Godwin to build *(p.72)* up so much power.

- He relied on Godwin's military support to help him keep control of England.
- He was married to Godwin's daughter, Edith, and family loyalty was important to the Anglo-Saxons.
- Godwin had helped Edward the Confessor to become king.
- Later, Edward the Confessor allowed the Godwin's family power to grow because he needed their help to protect England from the Norwegian threat, as well as from the Welsh.

What did Earl Godwin do?

Before his death in 1053, Godwin played an important role in the history of Anglo-Saxon England.

- He resisted the influence of Edward's Norman friends in England.
- He was exiled from England, but later returned.
- He put pressure on Edward the Confessor to agree to his plans.
- He built up the power of his family.

How was Godwin's relationship with the Normans?

He resisted the appointment of Normans to the nobility and the Church, and worked to get them sent home.

Why did Godwin go into exile?

In 1050, Godwin refused to punish the people of Dover after a deadly skirmish between visiting officials from Boulogne and townspeople. He was forced into exile as a result.

Why did Godwin return from exile?

In 1051, Godwin raised an army and pressured Edward into ending his exile and restoring his earldom.

How did Godwin increase the power of Godwin's family?

Godwin pressured Edward into giving important Church positions and earldoms to his sons and supporters.

Who were Godwin's rivals?

Few earls in England had the power to rival the Godwin family, but they were challenged by an alliance between Mercia and Wales.

- Aelfgar, Earl of Mercia, was the only earl with the power to challenge Godwin.
- Aelfgar worked with the Welsh king, Gruffudd ap Llywelyn.

How did the rivalry between Godwin and Aelfgar end?

After the death of Aelfgar, Harold and Tostig Godwinson launched a joint attack on Gruffudd and defeated him.

What was the significance of the Godwin family?

By 1060, the Godwin family had become very powerful and controlled much of England. Before 1066 they were at the centre of some significant events in Anglo-Saxon England.

- In 1051, Godwin returned from exile.
- In 1062, after the death of Aelfgar, the Godwinsons attacked Gruffudd, the Welsh king.
- In 1065, there was a rebellion *(p.35)* against Godwin's son, Tostig, in Northumbria.
- In 1064, Godwin's son Harold went on an official visit to Normandy.

Who was in the Godwin family?

One of the reasons for Godwin's power was his large family of sons. This gave him strong, loyal representatives in Anglo-Saxon England. Some of the most important members of the Godwin family were:

- Harold Godwinson.
- Tostig Godwinson.
- Gyrth Godwinson.
- Leofwine Godwinson.

Where did Godwin's son Harold rule?

Harold Godwinson became the Earl of Wessex after his father died.

Where did Godwin's son Tostig rule?

In 1055, Tostig Godwinson became the Earl of Northumbria, giving the Godwins a power base in the north of England.

Who did the Godwin family members marry?

The Godwin family made a series of politically helpful marriages that helped them to grow their power.

- Godwin's daughter, Edith, married Edward the Confessor.
- Harold married Edith the Fair, who owned large estates in East Anglia.
- Tostig married Judith, the daughter of the Count of Flanders.

DID YOU KNOW?

A big fight in Dover has international repercussions.

The retinue of Edward's brother-in-law, Eustace II, count of Boulogne, greatly offended the citizens of Dover by not paying for their lodgings. A scuffle developed and, apparently acting in self defence, a Dover resident killed one of the Normans – this led to retaliatory actions which resulted in several dead Saxons. The men of Dover then drove the Normans out of the town.

HAROLD GODWINSON

The life and career of Harold Godwinson, his claim to the throne, and his death at the Battle of Hastings.

Who was Harold Godwinson?

Harold Godwinson was the Earl of Wessex and the most powerful noble in England at the death of Edward the Confessor. He became King Harold II of England but lost the Battle of Hastings *(p.28)* to William, Duke of Normandy.

Who was Harold Godwinson's family?

Harold was part of the powerful Anglo-Saxon Godwin family.

- ✅ His father, Godwin, was a thegn who was made Earl of Wessex by King Cnut and grew very powerful.
- ✅ His brothers, including Tostig, Leofwine and Gyrth, were also powerful Anglo-Saxon earls.
- ✅ His wife, Edith the Fair, owned large amounts of land in East Anglia.

Where was Harold Godwinson based?

Harold was Earl of Wessex, a large area of land in the south of England.

What was Harold Godwinson's Norman Embassy?

In 1064, Harold travelled to Normandy, in an embassy on behalf of King Edward. It was a significant visit.

Why did Harold Godwinson go to Normandy?

Harold Godwinson travelled to see William, Duke of Normandy, in 1064 on a mission for King Edward. However, the exact reason for his visit is unclear.

- ✅ The Normans claimed that King Edward asked Harold to talk to William about succeeding him as king, and that Harold swore allegiance to William.
- ✅ The Anglo-Saxons claimed that Harold went to negotiate the release of his brother and nephew (Wulfnoth and Hakon), who were William's hostages.

What happened on Harold Godwinson's journey to Normandy?

Harold's journey to Normandy was eventful.

- ✅ He travelled to France, but was blown off course and landed at Ponthieu.
- ✅ He was taken prisoner by Count Guy of Ponthieu.
- ✅ William demanded that Count Guy hand Harold over to him.

What did Harold Godwinson do in Normandy?

Whilst in Normandy, Harold and William worked together fairly successfully. Harold performed a number of tasks for William.

- ✅ He stayed with William.
- ✅ He delivered Edward's message to William.
- ✅ He fought with William in two military campaigns.
- ✅ He received gifts of armour and weapons as a sign of William's gratitude.
- ✅ The Normans claimed that, by the end of the visit, Harold was prepared to take an oath of allegiance to William.

Did Harold Godwinson swear an oath to William?

While in Normandy, Harold made an oath to William, on two holy relics.

- ✅ The Normans claimed that this was an oath of allegiance, with Harold promising to support William's claim to the throne.
- ✅ However, while Harold did not dispute that he took an oath, he did not agree that he supported William's claim to the throne.

What was the significance of Harold Godwinson's visit to Normandy?

Harold's visit to William, and his oath, were significant for a number of reasons.

- ✅ It demonstrated how much Edward the Confessor trusted and relied on Harold.

- It showed how close England and Normandy were, which boosted William's claim to the throne.
- It allowed the Normans to claim that Harold was an oath-breaker when he took the throne after Edward's death.

Why did Harold Godwinson think he should be king?

Harold Godwinson, Earl of Wessex, had several reasons for claiming the throne when Edward the Confessor died in 1066.

- He was Edward's brother-in-law.
- He had great military power and a history of military success.
- He had influence and support among the earls and thegns.
- He had been the king's trusted advisor and right-hand man. He had even acted as 'sub regulus' (deputy king) for Edward.
- He claimed that Edward, on his deathbed, had nominated him to be king.

What were the strengths of Harold Godwinson's claim to the throne?

Harold Godwinson was one of the strongest claimants to the crown of England in 1066.

- He had the support of thegns, earls and the Witan in England. This gave him considerable support from the military power of England.
- He had been nominated as Edward's successor by the king himself, on his deathbed, and had witnesses to support his claim.

What were the weaknesses of Harold Godwinson's claim to the throne?

There were reasons why Harold's claim to the throne was opposed.

- William, duke of Normandy challenged his claim that Edward had wanted Harold as king.
- Harold wasn't related to the king by blood.

When did Harold Godwinson take power?

On 6th January 1066 - the day of Edward's burial - Harold Godwinson was crowned Harold II of England.

Why was Harold Godwinson made king in 1066?

Harold was, essentially, in the right place at the right time.

- He moved fast and seized his opportunity.
- The Witan agreed that he should be king.

Why did the Witan choose Harold Godwinson?

The Witan agreed that Harold Godwinson should become king on the 5th January 1066, the day of Edward's death. There were a number of reasons for this.

- They were already gathered for the opening of Westminster Abbey in London.
- They were aware of the threat from Normandy, and wanted a warrior king who could take swift action.
- They were likely to object to a Norman king - as Godwin had objected to Edward's Norman advisers.

What challenges did Harold Godwinson face as king?

As soon as he became king, Harold faced threats and challenges.

- Other English earls might not agree with the choice, particularly those from Mercia, which was Wessex's rival.
- Northumbria might not accept Tostig's brother as king.
- Tostig was in Europe, bitter and angry at Harold and looking for allies.

- ✓ William of Normandy was reported to be building *(p.72)* an invasion fleet.

 ## What did Harold Godwinson do after his coronation?

Immediately after his coronation, Harold took swift action to deal with the threats to his rule.

- ✓ He travelled to York, to ensure that he had the support of Northumbrian members of the Witan, who had not been in London. This was to ensure that the north would remain loyal.
- ✓ To strengthen his position, he married the sister of the earls Edwin and Morcar.
- ✓ He gathered a large army and fleet from the fyrd, and positioned them on the south coast of England to guard against an invasion from Normandy.
- ✓ He kept the army in one place all summer, until the autumn when it was time for them to stand down and return home.

 ## Which battles did Harold Godwinson fight in 1066?

In 1066, Harold Godwinson led his army into 2 significant battles:

- ✓ The Battle of Stamford Bridge *(p.26)* on 25th September, in which Harald Hardrada and Tostig Godwinson were defeated and killed.
- ✓ The Battle of Hastings *(p.28)* on 14th October, in which he was defeated and killed by the Norman army of William, Duke of Normandy.

 ## What did Harold Godwinson do once he was king in 1066?

Once he was king, Harold took decisive action to defend England from threats.

- ✓ He assembled his army on the south coast to wait for a Norman attack.
- ✓ He responded to news of a Viking attack by taking his army north to defeat Harald Hardrada at Stamford Bridge.
- ✓ He returned with his troops to London on hearing news of William's attack on the south.
- ✓ He led his troops out to meet the Norman army at Hastings.
- ✓ He fought and lost against William's Norman army at the Battle of Hastings *(p.30)* on 14th October 1066.

 ## What were Harold Godwinson's tactics in the Battle of Hastings?

At the Battle of Hastings *(p.28)*, the Anglo-Saxons' main tactic was to capture the high ground, and use the shield wall to form an impenetrable defensive position. This tactic depended on the shield wall holding in the face of attack.

 ## What advantages did Harold Godwinson have at Hastings?

Harold and the Anglo-Saxon army had some advantages at the Battle of Hastings *(p.28)*. Two of the most important were:

- ✓ Holding the high ground at the top of Senlac Hill.
- ✓ The shield wall.

 ## How did Harold Godwinson die?

Harold was killed at Hastings, possibly by an arrow in the eye. This was a random event that had a huge impact on the outcome of the battle.

DID YOU KNOW?

Harold was one of 11 children!

His sister Edith married the king, Edward the Confessor, and four of his six brothers went on the become earls, which meant that, by 1060, every earldom of England except Mercia was ruled by his family.

Quizzes, amazing exam preparation tools and more at GCSEHistory.com

THE SUCCESSION CRISIS

The contenders for the English throne after the death of Edward the Confessor.

What was the succession crisis of 1066?

After Edward the Confessor died on 5th January, 1066, there was a struggle for the throne of England between four men. The crisis ended with the Battle of Hastings *(p.28)* on 14th October, 1066.

Why were there different contenders for the throne after Edward the Confessor died?

Because Edward the Confessor was childless when he died, it wasn't clear who should succeed him as king. Several people claimed to be his rightful heir.

Which contenders had claims on the throne of England after Edward the Confessor's death?

Four people had claims to the throne of England.

- ✅ Harold Godwinson.
- ✅ Edgar Aetheling.
- ✅ Harald Hardrada, who was supported by Tostig Godwinson.
- ✅ William, duke of Normandy.

Which contender to the throne in 1066 had the strongest claim?

The contenders for the throne in 1066 all claimed the throne through family relationships. These were either blood relationships, or through marriage or other agreements.

- ✅ Edgar Aetheling was Edward the Confessor's closest blood relative - his great-nephew. He was called the Aetheling, which was a name that indicated an heir apparent.
- ✅ Harold Godwinson was Edward the Confessor's brother-in-law. His sister, Edith, was married to Edward.
- ✅ William, Duke of Normandy, was related to Edward the Confessor through his great-aunt, Emma of Normandy, who was Edward's mother.
- ✅ Harald Hardrada inherited the claim to the throne through an agreement between Harthacnut and Magnus, which Harald claimed extended to him.

Which contender to the throne in 1066 one had the strongest army?

The contenders for the throne in 1066 were supported by varying degrees of military power.

- ✅ Harold Godwinson had the support of the Witan, thegns and earls in England. This meant that he could raise an army of about 8,000 men, with potentially many more from the fyrd.
- ✅ William had years of military experience. He had a strong, skilled army of at least 7,000 men, including archers and cavalry.
- ✅ Harald Hardrada had a strong fleet of about 300 ships, and could raise as many as 10,000 soldiers.
- ✅ Edgar was fifteen when Edward died. He had no military experience, and no wealth. That meant he had little military support to defend the kingdom.

Which contender to the throne did Edward the Confessor choose?

Edward the Confessor's choice of successor after his death was a point of disagreement between the contenders.

- ✅ William, duke of Normandy claimed to have an agreement with Edward the Confessor, made in 1051, that he would inherit the throne if Edward died childless.
- ✅ The Anglo-Saxons claimed that, on his deathbed, Edward promised the crown to Harold Godwinson.
- ✅ Edgar's name 'Aetheling' was an Anglo-Saxon word meaning 'heir', but as he was a child when Edward died, it was unlikely that Edward saw him as the next king.

Harald Hardrada's claim bypassed Edward completely, and instead originated from King Harthacnut.

What alliances did the contenders to the throne have in 1066?

The contenders to the throne had important alliances in 1066.

 Harold Godwinson had the support of thegns, earls and Witan in England. They wanted a strong military leader, and so preferred his claim to Edgar Aetheling's.

 William had the support of the pope. He also claimed that Harold Godwinson had sworn to support his claim during his Normandy embassy of 1064.

 Harald Hardrada had the support of Tostig Godwinson, Harold's brother. There was also a possibility that he might be a popular choice in the Danelaw.

What nationality were the contenders to the throne in 1066?

Many of the Saxons disliked the idea of a foreign king. They had objected to the number of Normans that Edward had invited to England in the 1050s.

 Harold Godwinson and Edgar Aetheling were English.

 William, Duke of Normandy, was a Norman from a region of France.

 Harald Hardrada was the King of Norway.

HARALD HARDRADA

Harald Hardrada, the Norwegian king who claimed the English throne, and his death at the Battle of Stamford Bridge.

Who was Harald Hardrada?

Harald Hardrada was the King of Norway. In 1066 he invaded England in an attempt to take the throne.

Why did Harald Hardrada think he should be king?

There were a number of reasons why Harald Hardrada had a claim to the throne.

 His predecessor in Norway, Magnus, had made an agreement with Harthacnut, a previous Viking king of England.

 The agreement said that, if Harthacnut died before Magnus, then Magnus would succeed him as king of England.

 This had not happened, but as Magnus' successor in Norway, Harald believed that the agreement extended to him.

What were the strengths of Harald Hardrada's claim to the throne?

Harald Hardrada felt his claim was strong.

 He had succeeded to the Norwegian throne when Magnus died, so he felt that Magnus' agreement with Harthacnut extended to him.

 England had been ruled by Vikings from 1016 to 1042. Many Anglo-Danes lived in England, and might welcome another Viking king.

What were the weaknesses of Harald Hardrada's claim to the throne?

Harald Hardrada's claim was not, in fact, particularly strong.

 The agreement between Magnus and Harthacnut had been between the two kings, and it did not extend to their successors.

 Although many Anglo-Danes might have accepted Harald, most people in England did not want a Viking king.

- ☑ Harald had no other ties or relationship with England.
- ☑ There is no evidence that Harald intended to claim the throne until he was urged to do so by Tostig Godwinson in 1066.

How strong was Harald Hardrada?

In 1066, Harald was able to muster a fleet of 300 ships and up to 10,000 soldiers.

Who were Harald Hardrada's allies?

Harald Hardrada allied with Tostig Godwinson, Harold's brother.

What did Harald Hardrada do?

In September 1066 Harald Hardrada led a Viking invasion (p.26) on the north-east of England.

Which battles did Harald Hardrada fight in England?

During the Viking attack on England, Harald Hardrada was involved in two important battles:

- ☑ The Battle of Gate Fulford (p.25), in which he defeated the army of Anglo-Saxon earls Edwin and Morcar.
- ☑ The Battle of Stamford Bridge (p.26), against Harold Godwinson and his Anglo-Saxon army. Hardrada was defeated and killed in this battle.

DID YOU KNOW?

Some facts about Harald Hardrada.

- ✔ Hardrada means 'hard ruler'.
- ✔ In his younger days, Hardrada had served in the Varangian Guard in Constantinople. His boss was the Eastern Roman emperor.

EDGAR AETHELING

Edgar Aetheling, the royal prince who lost his bid to become king of England.

Who was Edgar Aetheling?

Edgar Aetheling was the great-nephew of Edward the Confessor. As Edward's closest male relative, he was a contender for the throne in 1066, and was later involved in rebellions against the Normans.

Why did Edgar Aetheling think he should be king?

Edgar Aetheling was Edward the Confessor's closest male relative, so he thought he had a good claim to the throne.

What were the strengths of Edgar Aetheling's claim to the throne?

Edgar Aetheling appeared to have a strong claim to the English throne.

- ☑ He was Edward the Confessor's closest blood relative - his great-nephew.
- ☑ His father, Edward the Exile, had been nominated to succeed Edward the Confessor, but had died before Edward. However, as the Exile's son, Edgar felt he should take his father's place.
- ☑ Edgar had been brought up by Edward the Confessor. He was called the Aetheling, which was a name that indicated an heir apparent.

What were the weaknesses of Edgar Aetheling's claim to the throne?

Edgar Aetheling's claim was not considered strong for a number of reasons.

- ✅ He was only around fifteen when Edward the Confessor died. The Witan thought he was too young to lead England when there were other stronger claimants who might invade.
- ✅ Edgar had no military experience, and no wealth. That meant he had little military support to defend the kingdom.
- ✅ There was no law that said that the throne should go to the previous king's closest male relative.
- ✅ Because he had been born in Hungary and had lived there for the first few years of his life, Edgar was not well known to the nobles.

 When was Edgar Aetheling crowned king?

Following Harold Godwinson's defeat at Hastings in October 1066, Edgar was hastily crowned king in London. However, he and other important Anglo-Saxon earls surrendered to William, Duke of Normandy shortly afterwards, at Berkhamsted.

 What rebellions was Edgar Aetheling involved in?

Edgar Aetheling was involved in a number of uprisings following the Norman conquest.

- ✅ He was involved in Edwin and Morcar's rebellion *(p.35)* of 1068.
- ✅ He led a rebellion *(p.35)* of Anglo-Saxons and Danish invaders in 1069.

DID YOU KNOW?

The last of the line.

Edgar remained unmarried and never produced any children. He lived until 1126, dying at 75. Edgar was the last living male member of the Anglo-Saxon royalty.

VIKING INVASION, 1066

Harald Hardrada's invasion of England in 1066.

 What was the Viking invasion in 1066?

In September 1066, Tostig and Hardrada launched an invasion on England.

 What did the invading Vikings do first in 1066?

The Viking attack came as a surprise to the English.

- ✅ Hardrada had about 300 ships in his fleet, and perhaps 10,000 Viking soldiers.
- ✅ They landed at the River Humber and marched up to York.
- ✅ At Gate Fulford *(p.25)*, outside York, they met an army led by Morcar, Earl of Northumbria and his brother Edwin, Earl of Mercia, who decided to meet the invaders outside the city *(p.67)*.

 What happened in the Viking invasion of England in 1066.

The Viking invasion *(p.26)* of 1066 involved two main battles.

- ✅ The Battle of Gate Fulford *(p.25)* against the brothers Edwin and Morcar, Earls of Mercia and Northumbria, was a resounding defeat for the Anglo-Saxons.

The Battle of Stamford Bridge *(p.26)*, against King Harold and his army, led to defeat for the Vikings.

BATTLE OF GATE FULFORD, 1066
The Battle of Gate Fulford, when Harald Hardrada defeated the Saxons.

What happened at the Battle of Gate Fulford?

The Battle of Gate Fulford was a crushing defeat for the Anglo-Saxons, who were led by Earls Edwin and Morcar.

Why did the Anglo-Saxons lose the battle of Gate Fulford?

There were a number of reasons why Edwin and Morcar were disadvantaged in the Battle of Gate Fulford.

- They might have been outnumbered. Although many Vikings stayed with the ships, Hardrada and Tostig's forces numbered up to 10,000. Edwin and Morcar are believed to have had 6,000 men.
- Harald Hardrada was a good tactician and an experienced warrior.
- Edwin and Morcar stationed their troops in front of marshland, leaving them nowhere to retreat.

What were the events of the Battle of Gate Fulford?

Hardrada positioned Tostig's weaker troops at one wing of his army.

- When the Anglo-Saxons charged them, Hardrada brought his stronger soldiers to attack them from the side.
- The English army broke and tried to retreat, but ran into the marsh and got stuck.
- The Vikings cut the Anglo-Saxons down, and claimed that they could avoid getting their boots muddy in the marsh by walking on the English corpses.
- Edwin and Morcar escaped from the slaughter, but it is very likely they were too weakened to play any role in the later battles of Stamford Bridge and Hastings.

How did Harold Godwinson react to the Viking invasion at the Battle of Gate Fulford?

When Harold learned of the Viking invasion *(p.26)* he brought his housecarls north to meet them.

- Harold learnt of the Viking invasion *(p.26)*, possibly through beacon signals, but did not know about the Battle of Gate Fulford.
- The southern fyrd, which had been disbanded on the 8th September, was recalled.

What did Harold's journey to the north involve in 1066 for the Battle of Gate Fulford?

Harold's army had a long journey in order to meet the Viking invaders in the north.

- On 20th September, Harold set off, leading his housecarls on the 185-mile journey north.
- He sent messages to gather a new army to travel ahead of him, gathering troops from East Anglia and Mercia.
- It isn't clear how Harold travelled north. It may have been on foot, but it is possible his army sailed up the coast.

BATTLE OF STAMFORD BRIDGE, 1066

The Battle of Stamford Bridge, when Harold Godwinson defeated Harald Hardrada's army and saved England from the Viking invasion.

What was the Battle of Stamford Bridge?

The Battle of Stamford Bridge was fought on 25th September, 1066, between Hardrada and Tostig's Viking invaders, and Harold Godwinson's Anglo-Saxon army.

What happened at the Battle of Stamford Bridge?

The Battle of Stamford Bridge was a victory for Harold's Anglo-Saxon army.

- ☑ Hardrada and Tostig had demanded hostages from all over Yorkshire, and were waiting for them at Stamford Bridge.
- ☑ Harold and his army launched a surprise attack on the Vikings from behind a small hill overlooking Stamford Bridge.
- ☑ Hardrada and Tostig were both killed, and it was reported that only 24 Viking ships (out of the original 300) returned home.

Why did Harold win the Battle of Stamford Bridge?

Harold had several military advantages at the Battle of Stamford Bridge.

- ☑ The Vikings had left their armour on their ships as it was a hot day, along with around a third of their men.
- ☑ Harold took Hardrada and Tostig completely by surprise, as they had not expected him to arrive in the north so quickly.
- ☑ Hardrada's army had recently fought a battle, and were not expecting another so soon.
- ☑ Harold's housecarls showed endurance and skill in breaking the Viking shield wall.

DID YOU KNOW?

The Battle of Stamford Bridge has nothing to do with Chelsea FC!

The Stamford Bridge stadium was named after a bridge next to the ground, originally called 'Samfordesbrigge' - literally, the 'bridge at the sandy ford'.

SIGNIFICANCE OF THE VIKING INVASION

The significance of the Saxon victory at Stamford Bridge, and its implications for the future of England.

What was the significance of the Viking invasion of England?

The Viking defeat helped the Norman invasion to succeed.

How did the Viking invasion help the Normans?

The Viking invasion meant that Harold's army wasn't waiting on the south coast when the Normans landed in late September 1066. Unfortunately, the fyrd had already been disbanded before Harold's army marched north.

Did the Viking invasion make much difference to Harold's army at Hastings?

Although Harold had been victorious, he had lost men at both Gate Fulford *(p.25)* and Stamford Bridge. These included the professional housecarls. As a result, he could call on fewer experienced warriors to fight against William's Norman army.

 ### Did Edwin and Morcar fight at the Battle of Hastings after losing against the Vikings invasion?

Edwin and Morcar do not appear in the records of the Battle of Hastings *(p.28)*. It could be that they refused - or were not in a position - to fight after their defeat, but it could also be that they just weren't mentioned.

How tired were Harold's troops after defeating the Viking invasion?

Harold's recent battle and march south must have exhausted his housecarls. However, after their great victory, morale would have been high.

DID YOU KNOW?

Without Hardrada's aggression, modern England could have been very different.

It is unquestionable that if Harold had not been distracted and diverted by the battles in the north, then he would have been better prepared to fight William at Hastings and he might have repelled the Normans. We might be speaking a totally different language, for a start!

THE NORMAN THREAT

The extent of the threat of William of Normandy to England, and Harold's efforts to contain it.

 ### What was the Norman threat to England in 1066?

Since Harold's coronation, reports had informed him that William, Duke of Normandy was preparing an invasion fleet. Harold had stationed an army and a fleet on the south coast, but by September this had been disbanded.

 ### Why did Harold leave England unprotected against the Norman threat in 1066?

Events showed that abandoning the south coast to face the Vikings was not a good decision for Harold to make. However, he had a number of reasons for doing so.

- ☑ The fyrd needed to return home and look after their farms and families, and to gather the harvest.
- ☑ The Viking invasion *(p.26)* presented a more immediate threat.
- ☑ The September storms had wrecked some of Harold's ships, and had probably affected William's in the same way.
- ☑ There was a strong northerly wind that prevented the Normans from sailing when originally planned.
- ☑ It was difficult to keep a standing army for a long time, and Harold knew that William must have faced the same difficulties that he had.

 ### How did Harold respond to the Norman threat in 1066?

Harold faced the Norman threat by gathering a huge army and fleet from the fyrd on the south coast. However, in September this was disbanded, and Harold marched north to deal with the Vikings.

When was the Norman threat finally realised in 1066?

On 1st October, 1066, less than a week after the Battle of Stamford Bridge *(p.26)*, King Harold received word that William and the Norman army had landed on the south coast on 28th September.

BATTLE OF HASTINGS, 1066

The Battle of Hastings, 14 October 1066.

 ### What was the Battle of Hastings?

The Battle of Hastings took place between the armies of William, Duke of Normandy and Harold Godwinson, king of England. It was a victory for the Normans.

 ### When was the Battle of Hastings?

The Battle of Hastings took place on 14th October, 1066.

 ### What happened at the Battle of Hastings?

The exact events of the Battle of Hastings are unclear, but some things are known.

- William was aware of Harold's approach and there was a dash for the top of the hill, which the Anglo-Saxons won. Gaining the higher ground gave the Anglo-Saxons an advantage.
- The Anglo-Saxons formed a shield wall at the top of the hill, which the Norman archers could not break. William sent his foot soldiers up the hill, followed by his cavalry, but they could not break the wall.
- At one point, a rumour went round the Norman troops that William had been killed. He lifted his helmet to show his face and rally them.
- Harold's shield wall was weakened when some Anglo-Saxons broke ranks to chase the retreating Normans. The Normans continued to reduce the shield wall until the remainder was broken.

 ### How did the Battle of Hastings end?

With the shield wall broken, the Norman cavalry charged the Anglo-Saxons. Harold Godwinson, his brothers Gyrth and Leofwine and most of their housecarls were killed. The remaining troops fled.

 ### What armies did Harold Godwinson and William have at the Battle of Hastings?

The fact that the Battle of Hastings lasted all day suggests that the two armies were fairly evenly matched. Both had a core of well-trained, well-equipped men, alongside ordinary soldiers.

- William is thought to have had about 4,000-6,000 troops, with about 800 elite knights. His army included cavalry and archers.
- Harold led about 6,000-7,000 soldiers, some of whom were housecarls.

 ### How did the Anglo-Saxons use the shield wall at the Battle of Hastings?

The shield wall at the top of the hill protected the Anglo-Saxon army against arrows and the Norman cavalry. While it remained disciplined, it was very difficult to break.

- It involved setting troops out in several close-set, parallel lines. The men at the front overlapped their shields and stuck their spears through the gaps.
- The shield wall formed a strong defensive position, effective against archers and difficult even for cavalry to break.
- It relied on discipline of the troops to hold the line.

☑ It was an effective tactic that had been used by Harald Hardrada at the Battle of Gate Fulford *(p.25)*.

What were the advantages of the higher ground in the Battle of Hastings?

Holding the higher ground was an advantage for the Anglo-Saxons. The Norman cavalry could not charge uphill at the strength needed to break the shield wall, and archers struggled to shoot up at Harold's troops.

How did the different sorts of soldiers help William in the Battle of Hastings?

The Norman troops had a variety of skills and tactics, while the Anglo-Saxons tended to fight in a similar way every time. This meant that William could try different methods of attack until he found one that worked.

How did the cavalry help the Norman army win the Battle of Hastings?

The Norman cavalry was a deadly force, with a strong charge and a height advantage in combat. Once the shield wall was broken, they devastated the Anglo-Saxon troops.

Why were the archers an advantage in the Battle of Hastings?

Once the shield wall was broken and the Norman archers could get closer to the Anglo-Saxon troops, they were able to cause great damage from a distance. Harold may have been killed by an arrow to the eye.

Did discipline make a difference in the Battle of Hastings?

The discipline of the Norman troops meant that they continued to form co-ordinated attacks using a variety of tactics, while the lack of discipline in the Anglo-Saxon army led to the breaking of the shield wall.

What was the feigned retreat tactic that William used at the Battle of Hastings?

During the battle the Normans feigned (faked) a retreat, causing the fyrd to break the shield wall and run down the hill to give chase. William's cavalry then doubled back and cut them down. This happened three times.

How did experimenting with battle tactics help William in the Battle of Hastings?

After his cavalry and archers' attacks on the Saxon position failed, William was able to use the feigned retreat to weaken the shield wall. Once it was weakened, he then deployed his archers and cavalry to break it completely.

How important was luck at the Battle of Hastings?

Although both the Anglo-Saxons and Normans had their strengths and weaknesses, the outcome of Hastings was also influenced by luck and chance. This was seen as 'God's will' by people at the time.

☑ Harold was killed at Hastings, possibly by an arrow in the eye. This was a random event that gave William victory.

☑ Harold was unlucky that the Vikings attacked shortly before the Normans sailed. Even though Harold had already disbanded the fyrd, this put the Anglo-Saxon troops at a disadvantage and meant they were exhausted by the time they arrived at Hastings.

☑ The weather was bad enough to damage the English fleet and to convince Harold that William wouldn't strike, but not bad enough to stop the Normans from sailing to England.

DID YOU KNOW?

Three facts about the Battle of Hastings.

✓ There is some disagreement about exactly where the battle took place. The traditional site was known as Senlac Hill; but there is a recent theory that it was actually fought at nearby Caldbec Hill.

✓ The battle was actually fought around 7 miles from Hastings, near the modern town of Battle. (The town was named after the battle, obviously.)

✓ In the 1070s a huge embroidery, known as the Bayeux Tapestry, was created to show the events of the battle. It is 68 metres long!

ARMIES AND TACTICS AT THE BATTLE OF HASTINGS

The Norman and Saxon armies at Hastings, and the tactics used by William and Harold.

How was the Battle of Hastings fought by the armies?

The two sides in the Battle of Hastings *(p.28)* fought with different tactics and in different styles.

What was the Norman army like at the Battle of Hastings?

William's army consisted of knights on horseback, archers, and infantry (footmen).

What were the Norman archers like in the Battle of Hastings?

Norman archers had padded jackets, called gambesons, as armour. They included crossbowmen.

What were the Norman knights like in the Battle of Hastings?

Knights were William's elite troops. They were skilled, well-equipped, and fought on horseback.

☑ Their weapons included lances, javelins, swords and maces.

☑ War-horses were called destriers. They were especially bred to be strong enough to carry an armoured knight *(p.56)*, and trained to be vicious in battle.

☑ Their shields were kite-shaped to protect the left side.

☑ Their armour was chain mail, and they wore a conical helmet with a nose-piece.

☑ Saddles held the knights in place to free their arms for fighting, while stirrups allowed them to stand up for extra power in attacks. Spurs were used to direct their horses in manoeuvres.

☑ Knights carried a gonfanon, a flag to signal manoeuvres.

☑ Knights spent years training to fight effectively on horseback.

What was the Norman infantry like at the Battle of Hastings?

The infantry, or foot-soldiers, of the Norman army probably had chain mail, shields, swords and javelins.

What was the Anglo-Saxon army like at the Battle of Hastings?

It is not known how many housecarls Harold brought to the Battle of Hastings *(p.28)*, but the Anglo-Saxon army had a well-trained, well-equipped core, along with the men of the fyrd.

What were the Anglo-Saxon housecarls like at the Battle of Hastings?

The housecarls were the elite of the Anglo-Saxon army. They were formidable soldiers who fought on foot.

- They were armed with swords, javelins, and long heavy axes.
- They carried a round wooden shield, with a metal boss in the centre for reinforcement.
- Housecarls were trained to open gaps in the shield wall for axe blows, then to close it up again. They were skilled with their axes and had great strength, discipline, and endurance.
- Their armour was chain mail, or metal plates sewn onto leather. They also had a conical helmet with a nose-piece.

Who were the Anglo-Saxon fyrd at the Battle of Hastings?

Harold had had to call the fyrd quickly as he marched back south, and some had not turned up on time, possibly including his own archers. The thegns had proper weapons, but many of the fyrd were armed only with farm tools.

Why did the Anglo-Saxon army not have horses at the Battle of Hastings?

The Norman cavalry turned out to be an advantage in the Battle of Hastings (p.28), but there were a number of reasons why the Anglo-Saxons did not fight on horseback.

- Instead of horses, the Anglo-Saxons invested in their fleet, and in fortifying towns against attacks from the sea. This was based on long experience of dealing with Viking invasions.
- The Norman cavalry was the result of years of breeding horses, training knights, and developing technology such as the saddle and lance. Developing good cavalry was difficult, expensive and time-consuming.

THE ENGLISH SURRENDER IN 1066

The aftermath of the Battle of Hastings, and the surrender of the Saxon lords.

What was the surrender of the English after the Battle of Hastings?

Within a few weeks of Harold Godwinson's defeat at the Battle of Hastings (p.28), the other earls of England had surrendered to William's rule. However, at first it seemed as though they might continue to fight.

What happened in the surrender of the Anglo-Saxons after the Battle of Hastings?

After the Battle of Hastings (p.28), the Anglo-Saxons in London looked as though they might continue the fight.

- Surviving troops from Hastings fled to London, where they met with the reinforcements from the fyrd, who had not arrived at Hastings in time.
- The Witan elected Edgar Aetheling as king. The Archbishops Stigand of Canterbury and Ealdred of York crowned him, and he was also supported by Edwin and Morcar.
- Edwin and Morcar sent their sister and Harold's widow, Ealdgyth, to Chester for safety.

How did William cause the English surrender after the Battle of Hastings?

William had a number of priorities following his victory at the Battle of Hastings (p.28).

- He secured the south coast, so that supplies and more troops could be sent from Normandy, although he and many of his army became ill at Dover.
- He sent soldiers to seize the royal treasury at Winchester.
- He then headed to London to force a surrender, destroying people's homes as he went.
- Instead of directly approaching heavily-fortified London, he first went north-west to Berkhamsted.

Who surrendered to William in 1066 after the Battle of Hastings?

At Berkhamsted, Edgar Aetheling met William, along with Archbishop Ealdred, Edwin, Morcar, and other leading earls. They surrendered to William, swore oaths to obey him, gave him hostages, and offered him the crown.

> **DID YOU KNOW?**
>
> The Normans pillaged and burnt many towns on their way north, including Romney in Kent.
>
> Romney was part destroyed because it had killed some Norman soldiers who had landed there in error when the original invasion fleet had crossed from Normandy.

WILLIAM'S REWARDS TO HIS FOLLOWERS

William had persuaded his followers to fight for him. Now he was in control of England, he had to reward his loyal followers.

Did William I reward his followers?

William I rewarded his supporters generously.

Why did William reward his followers?

William needed to reward his army, as they had travelled to England to fight for him, and had won him a great victory. He also needed their continued support to prevent trouble from the Anglo-Saxons.

How did William gain the land and money for rewards after 1066?

William gained the land and money to reward his supporters in various ways.

- ✅ He confiscated the royal treasury at Winchester.
- ✅ He set a heavy tax to raise funds from the Anglo-Saxons.
- ✅ He declared that all of the land in England belonged to him. He also took land off anyone who had fought against him at Hastings.

How did William I reward his Norman supporters?

William had persuaded Normans and mercenaries to join his army with the promise of wealth if they won.

- ✅ He kept about a fifth of the Godwinsons' and Edward's lands for himself, but granted the rest of it to his followers.
- ✅ His half-brother Odo, Bishop of Bayeux, received all of Kent.
- ✅ William FitzOsbern, William's relative and advisor, was granted large areas of Hampshire and the west, along with the Isle of Wight.
- ✅ Roger de Montgomery, who ruled Normandy while William was away, was made Earl of Shrewsbury. He also received land in Essex and Sussex.

How did William reward his Anglo-Saxon supporters?

The Anglo-Saxons who swore loyalty to William hoped for a share in the Godwin family's lands, but that went to William's supporters.

- ✅ Earls such as Edwin and Morcar were allowed to keep their earldoms.

Quizzes, amazing exam preparation tools and more at GCSEHistory.com

- ☑ Bishops such as Ealdred kept their positions.
- ☑ The Northumbrian Gospatric was made earl of northern Northumbria after paying a heavy tax to William.
- ☑ William also gained support by promising marriage alliances. For example, he promised that Edwin could marry his daughter.

THE MARCHER EARLDOMS

The Marcher earldoms were created to help protect Norman England from attacks by the Welsh and the Scots.

What were the Marcher earldoms?

The Marcher earldoms were new earldoms created by William along the border of Wales, to prevent the threat of Welsh attacks that Edward the Confessor had suffered.

Where were the Marcher earldoms?

The Marcher earldoms were created on the Welsh frontier.

- ☑ The earldom of Chester was created next to north Wales.
- ☑ The earldom of Shrewsbury was situated alongside the Welsh midlands.
- ☑ The earldom of Hereford was adjacent to south Wales.

Who were the Marcher earldoms awarded to?

William awarded the Marcher earldoms to some of his closest supporters and advisers.

- ☑ Hugh d'Avranches, whose father had contributed 60 ships to William's fleet, was made Earl of Chester.
- ☑ Roger de Montgomery, who ruled Normandy while William was away, was made Earl of Shrewsbury.
- ☑ William's right-hand man, William FitzOsbern, was made Earl of Hereford.

What was significant about the size of the Marcher earldoms?

The Marcher earldoms were smaller than Anglo-Saxon earldoms, which made them easier to control, but also meant that the Marcher earls were not as powerful and important as the king.

What rights did the Marcher earldoms have?

The Marcher earls could establish Norman churches instead of Anglo-Saxon ones, and create towns (boroughs) and markets. These were powers normally reserved only for the king. They encouraged Normans to move into the areas.

What laws could the Marcher earldoms make?

The sheriffs in the Marcher earldoms were answerable to the earl, rather than directly to the king. This gave the Marcher earls almost complete control over the courts and law and order in their regions.

What taxes did they pay in the Marcher earldoms?

Unlike other English earls, Marcher earls did not have to pay tax to the king on their land. This was a reward for loyalty, but also to encourage development of towns and defences.

What happened with castles in the Marcher earldoms?

Unlike the rest of England, the Marcher earls could build *(p. 72)* castles wherever they were needed, without asking permission from the king. This meant that they could control the area and attack the Welsh if necessary.

How powerful were the Marcher earldoms?

The Marcher earls controlled the frontier and had the autonomy to deal with trouble quickly and decisively. However, they still owed allegiance to the king, had to provide military service for him, and could not try people for high treason.

DID YOU KNOW?

They built many castles to help control the Welsh.

The Welsh Marches had the densest concentration of motte-and-bailey castles, in order to subdue the Welsh, a process that took William more than two centuries.

CASTLES

The Norman use of castles was an important factor in the way they demonstrated their power and control over England.

What were castles like in Norman times?

It is estimated that William built as many as 1,000 castles as a way of keeping control in England.

What were motte and bailey castles like?

The earliest Norman castles were known as motte and bailey castles. The motte was a large mound of earth that was topped with a keep, a wooden tower. The motte was surrounded by a bailey that contained the stables, barracks and kitchens.

What type of castles did the Normans build?

The Normans initially built motte and bailey castles. As time went on these were gradually rebuilt in stone.

Where were Norman castles built?

Castles were built in strategic locations such as key transport routes. They were also located where there was more likely to be unrest, so there were many castles on the Welsh frontier, as well as in Exeter, York and Nottingham.

What were the features of a motte and bailey castle?

Norman castles were known as motte and bailey castles, after their two key features - the motte and the bailey.

 The motte was a large mound of earth, about five to seven metres high.

 The keep was a strong wooden tower on top of the motte, that served as a lookout, an archers' stronghold, and the most secure defensive position in the castle.

The keep was accessed by steps cut into the motte, or a bridge.

 The bailey surrounded the motte and contained the stables, barracks and kitchens.

The bailey was protected by a strong wooden fence called a palisade.

 A deep ditch surrounded the bailey and the motte. Sometimes this was filled with water.

Entry to the castle was controlled by a gatehouse.

 Sometimes a drawbridge was built over the ditch, which could be drawn up in case of an attack.

What were the advantages of Norman castles?

Motte and bailey castles had several advantages for the Normans.

- ☑ They were relatively quick and easy to build *(p.72)*. With peasant labour, they could be constructed within weeks. Basic fortifications could even be completed within days, if necessary.

- ☑ They were new in England (although common in Normandy and other parts of Europe), which made them unfamiliar and intimidating to the Anglo-Saxons.

- ☑ They served as a symbol of Norman power.

- ☑ They provided a secure base for the lord and his soldiers.

 What were the effects of Norman castles?

Castles had a huge effect on the surrounding areas.

- ☑ They dominated the skyline and intimidated the Anglo-Saxons living nearby.

- ☑ In troublesome areas, they were spaced 20 miles apart. Norman soldiers could march 20 miles in a day, so this allowed them to deal with unrest quickly.

- ☑ Tens or hundreds of Anglo-Saxon homes might be destroyed to build *(p.72)* them - especially in towns - and local labour was used to build them.

DID YOU KNOW?

Windsor Castle in Berkshire was originally built around 1070. It is the longest continuously-occupied palace in Europe.

REBELLIONS AGAINST WILLIAM

Despite his victory at Hastings, it took William some years to fully pacify his new kingdom. He had to face a number of rebellions by his Saxon subjects.

 What were the Anglo-Saxons rebellions against the Normans?

As William attempted to establish control over England, many Anglo-Saxons weren't prepared to accept Norman rule. In several places, this discontent turned into rebellion, where the people rose up and fought against the Normans.

 When were the main Anglo-Saxon rebellions against the Normans?

There were a number of Anglo-Saxon rebellions against William while he was establishing control over England in the years 1066-1071.

- ☑ Rebellions in Kent, Northumbria, and on the Welsh border, in 1067.

- ☑ A rebellion in Exeter in 1068. William besieged Exeter, and prevented a further outbreak by granting the rebels concessions.

- ☑ A major rebellion in the north, led by Edwin and Morcar, in 1068.

- ☑ A major rebellion in the north, led by Edgar Aetheling, in 1069.

- ☑ A major rebellion in East Anglia, led by Hereward the Wake, in 1070-71.

EDWIN AND MORCAR'S REBELLION, 1068

Even though he allowed the Saxon earls Edwin and Morcar to keep their land and titles, William still had to deal with the brothers' 1068 rebellion.

What was Edwin and Morcar's rebellion?

In 1067, William returned to Normandy, taking with him Edwin, Morcar, Edgar Aetheling and other Anglo-Saxon lords, as well as English treasure. On their return in 1068, Edwin and Morcar fled north and led a rebellion *(p.35)* against William.

When was the rebellion of Edwin and Morcar?

Edwin and Morcar rebelled in the year 1068.

What was the importance of Edwin and Morcar's rebellion?

This was the first major rebellion *(p.35)* against William. It encouraged the next phase of rebellions, which led to William using more brutal methods to crush subsequent revolts.

What were the causes of Edwin and Morcar's rebellion?

There were five main reasons why the lords rebelled.

- ☑ Edwin and Morcar were unhappy about the land that they had lost under William.
- ☑ The English lords who went with William to Normandy were resentful when they returned - perhaps because they realised that English wealth would be used to benefit Normandy.
- ☑ They resented William's heavy geld tax.
- ☑ They resented the castles that the Normans had built across England.
- ☑ They were alarmed by the brutality of Norman rule.

Why did Edwin lead the rebellion against the Normans with Morcar?

Edwin, Earl of Mercia, had 2 main complaints against William.

- ☑ His earldom in Mercia had been made smaller and less important than it previously had been.
- ☑ William had gone back on his promise that Edwin could marry his daughter.

Why did Morcar lead a rebellion against William I with Edwin?

Morcar had three main reasons for rebelling:

- ☑ Morcar resented the reduction of his landholding in Northumbria, and with it, his money and power.
- ☑ Parts of Northumbria had been given to one of Tostig's thegns, Copsig, who had submitted to William's rule.
- ☑ Control over parts of Yorkshire had been granted to Maerleswein.

How did land loss cause Edwin and Morcar's rebellion?

The Normans who had come to England with William took land from the Anglo-Saxons, which William allowed.

How did Norman brutality cause Edwin and Morcar's rebellion?

Odo and William FitzOsbern had unlawfully seized lands, and their soldiers had been allowed to behave brutally, even raping Anglo-Saxon women.

Why did resentment over castles lead to Edwin and Morcar's rebellion in 1069?

Norman castles were resented for several reasons:

- [x] They represented Norman power and control.
- [x] They often involved the destruction of Anglo-Saxon homes.
- [x] The Normans commandeered resources from the surrounding areas to build *(p.72)* the castles.

Why did Norman taxes lead to Edwin and Morcar's rebellion in 1069?

The heavy geld tax that William introduced in late 1066 was resented.

Who was involved in Edwin and Morcar's rebellion?

The 1068 rebellion *(p.35)* in the north involved a number of Anglo-Saxon lords.

- [x] Brothers Edwin, Earl of Mercia, and Morcar, Earl of Northumbria, were its leaders.
- [x] Bleddyn, Lord of Powys in Wales.
- [x] Maerleswein, Sheriff of Yorkshire.
- [x] Earl Waltheof and Earl Gospatric of Northumbria.
- [x] Edgar Aetheling, great-nephew of Edward the Confessor.

How did William respond to Edwin and Morcar's rebellion in 1068 - 1069?

William responded to the rebellion *(p.35)* swiftly, with a show of great force.

- [x] He went north with his army, building *(p.72)* castles as they marched.
- [x] They went to Warwick, a key town *(p.67)* in Mercia, and built a castle there.
- [x] They also built a castle in Nottingham.

How did the rebels react after Edwin and Morcar's rebellion?

The rebellion *(p.35)* disintegrated quickly when William took action.

- [x] Edwin and Morcar surrendered after William took control of Warwick. William pardoned them, but kept them at his court where he could keep an eye on them. They escaped again in 1071.
- [x] York sent hostages to William after he took Nottingham, as did the Northumbrian rebels.
- [x] Edgar and other rebel leaders fled to Malcolm III in Scotland.

Why did Edwin and Morcar's rebellion fail?

There are a number of possible reasons why Edwin and Morcar's rebellion *(p.35)* failed.

- [x] It may have been a test to see how William responded. The rebels could have been waiting for a better opportunity.
- [x] It is possible that the rebels were not clear or united about what they wanted. Edwin and Morcar may have just wanted their land back.
- [x] The escape of rebel leaders, including Edgar Aetheling, to Scotland, created a new rebel base which was important in 1069.
- [x] Ultimately, William's show of force and efficient castle-building was an effective way of regaining control.

DID YOU KNOW?

Edwin was not popular among his retinue.

During Hereward the Wake's rebellion in East Anglia in 1071 Edwin was betrayed to the Normans by his own retinue and murdered.

EDGAR AETHELING'S REBELLION, 1069

Edgar Aetheling continued to challenge William, and led a rebellion against Norman rule in 1069.

What was Edgar Aetheling's rebellion in 1069?

In 1069 there was another rebellion *(p.35)* against William, led by Edgar Aetheling, which started with the murder of Robert Cumin, one of William's supporters.

Who led the Edgar Aetheling rebellion in 1069?

Edgar Aetheling, great-nephew of Edward the Confessor, led the rebellion *(p.35)*, but he was joined by others.

- Malcolm III of Scotland, who was married to Edgar's sister, supported him.
- King Sweyn of Denmark sent a fleet and army, led by his brother Asbjorn, which joined Edgar.

What was important about Edgar Aetheling's rebellion of 1069?

Edgar's rebellion *(p.35)* was important because it led to the Harrying of the North and marked a change in William's strategy in dealing with rebellions.

Why was Robert Cumin killed in Edgar Aetheling's rebellion of 1069?

One of the rebels' targets was Robert Cumin, a supporter of William.

- William chose Cumin to replace Gospatric as earl of northern Northumbria, after Gospatric's betrayal in 1068.
- Cumin and a large force of his men attacked and looted towns in northern Northumbria in January 1069.
- The Bishop of Durham warned Cumin that this would cause resentment, but Cumin ignored him.
- A group of Northumbrians surprised Cumin's men, and killed them in the streets of Durham.
- Cumin hid in the bishop's house, but the rebels set fire to it, and killed him when he ran out.

What happened in York during Edgar Aetheling's rebellion of 1068 - 1069?

Shortly after the murder of Robert Cumin, there was a similar revolt *(p.35)* in York.

- The uprising *(p.35)* began when rebels killed the Norman governor of York and many Norman soldiers.
- They were joined by Edgar Aetheling and his rebels from Scotland.

How did William react to the uprising in York in Edgar Aetheling's rebellion of 1068 - 1069?

William took a large army to York very quickly in February, and dealt with the rebellion *(p.35)* there.

- His troops devastated York as they hunted for the rebels.
- Edgar Aetheling escaped back to Scotland.
- William built a new castle, and put William FitzOsbern in charge of it.
- He then returned to Winchester for Easter celebrations.

How did the Vikings get involved in Edgar Aetheling's rebellion of 1068 - 1069?

In September 1069, William's troubles worsened when a Danish force joined Edgar's Anglo-Saxon rebels and looted York.

- The Viking forces that joined Edgar's rebellion *(p.35)* in 1069 increased the pressure on William's rule.
- King Sweyn of Denmark assembled a large fleet..
- The Danes raided the east coast, meeting up with Edgar's troops and co-ordinating their attacks.
- The combined army marched on York.
- The Norman army accidentally set the city *(p.67)* on fire in their attempts to defend it.

- They then went out to meet the Anglo-Danish rebels, and were slaughtered.
- Both castles in York were destroyed and the Danish ships sailed home full of English riches.
- As William travelled the north hunting down the rebels, news of other rebellions came from Shrewsbury and Chester.

Why did Edgar Aetheling's rebellion of 1069 fail?

Although William's rule was under pressure, the Normans managed to maintain power, for a number of reasons.

- The rebels retreated when William led troops into an area.
- The Anglo-Danish army split up after reaching York, instead of marching south.
- William was able to stop the Viking attacks by paying off the Danes.

Was William worried by the Danes during Edgar Aetheling's rebellion of 1068 -1069?

The Danes were a worry for William, for a variety of reasons.

- They were far more experienced sailors than the Normans.
- There was a possibility that they would be more welcome in the Danelaw than the Normans were.
- William believed that they would keep raiding and then retreating until the Norman troops were exhausted.

How did William react to the Viking rebels during Edgar Aetheling's rebellion of 1069?

William marched his troops up north to put down the Anglo-Danish rebellion *(p.35)*, but the rebels fled. He therefore changed his tactics.

- He paid the Danes a large sum of money to leave.
- He began a campaign of total destruction in the north of England - the 'Harrying of the North'.

THE HARRYING OF THE NORTH, 1069-1070

Three years after Hastings, William had had enough of rebellious Saxons. In the winter of 1069-70 he decided to show them exactly what the price of rebellion was.

What was the Harrying of the North?

'Harrying' means to devastate a place. In 1069, William decided to deal with uprisings in the north with an event that became known as 'The Harrying of the North'. Norman soldiers stormed villages, killing many people, burning fields, and destroying livestock and food stores.

When was the Harrying of the North?

The Harrying of the North began in the winter of 1069 and continued into 1070.

What was the importance of the Harrying of the North?

The Harrying of the North was important because it marked a turning point in William's strategy for dealing with rebellions. The consequences made it difficult to continue resistance against William.

Why did the Normans harry the north?

It is possible that William ordered the Harrying of the North in a fit of rage - there is evidence that he regretted it afterwards. However, at the time there were several other reasons for his decision.

- Many Normans, including the Norman earl Robert Cumin, had been killed by rebels.

- The guerrilla tactics of the rebels meant that William was unable to meet them in open battle. Instead, they took refuge in nearby villages. The Harrying of the North made this impossible.
- The Danish heritage of Anglo-Saxons in the north meant that their loyalty might be swayed by Danish invaders.
- The rebellions in the north triggered other rebellions across England.

 What were the short-term effects of the Harrying of the North?

The effects of the Harrying of the North in the short-term were horrific. An estimated 100,000 to 150,000 people were either killed, died of starvation in the resulting famine, or were displaced as refugees to other parts of the kingdom.

 What were the long-term effects of the Harrying of the North?

The effects of the Harrying of the North lasted for many years.

- There were no further uprisings in Northumbria.
- 16 years later, the Domesday Book (p.64) showed that one third of Yorkshire remained wasteland, and that there were as many as 150,000 fewer people in the area.
- The Danes no longer used the Danelaw as a beachhead for their invasions, and instead attacked in East Anglia.
- William decided to replace the remaining Anglo-Saxon nobility, rather than trying to work with them any more.
- The Harrying was widely criticised, including by the pope. William gave a lot of time and money to the Church as penance (to make amends) for his actions.

 How many people were killed in the Harrying of the North?

It is unsure how many people were killed or died of starvation as a result of the Harrying of the North, but estimates range between 80,000 and 100,000 people.

DID YOU KNOW?

Facts about the Harrying of the North.

✔ The Anglo-Norman writer, Orderic Vitalis, said that 100,000 people were killed or starved to death in the Harrying of the North. This was as much as 5% of the population.

✔ Fifteen years later, one third of Yorkshire was still described as 'waste'.

THE EAST ANGLIAN REVOLT, 1070-1

Despite the destruction of the Harrying of the North, William faced a new rebellion in 1070-1, this time in East Anglia.

What was the rebellion of Hereward the Wake?

After the Harrying of the North, Hereward the Wake began a rebellion (p.35) in the Fens of East Anglia, supported by the Danes who had returned to England.

When was the rebellion of Hereward the Wake?

Hereward the Wake was active against the Normans in 1070, which is when the uprising (p.35) at Ely occurred.

Who was involved in the 1070 uprising?

The 1070 uprising in Ely was another Anglo-Viking uprising (p.35).

- King Sweyn led his Danish fleet back to England.
- He made an alliance with a local rebel leader called Hereward the Wake.

 ### Why did Hereward the Wake rebel?

Hereward had been a local thegn who fought abroad, before coming home to find that his land had been given to a Norman lord.

- The Bishop of Peterborough had been replaced by a Norman called Turold.
- Hereward and the other East Anglian rebels fought a guerrilla war against the Normans.

 ### Where was the 1070 rebellion?

The rising in 1070-1071 was centred in Ely, in the Fens of East Anglia.

 ### How did William deal with guerrilla warfare during the rebellion of Hereward the Wake?

William had a number of methods for dealing with the guerrilla tactics of the rebels.

- He responded rapidly with a large force to stamp out resistance.
- He put trusted supporters in place to keep control of areas, once rebellions had been stamped out.
- He established castles in troubled areas.
- Ultimately, he decided that the remaining Anglo-Saxon lords needed to be removed from power.
- As a sign of desperation, however, William was said to have employed a witch to curse Hereward.
- As he had in 1069, William paid large sums of money to the Danish invaders to go away.

 ### How did William deal with discontent during the rebellion of 1070?

William dealt with unhappy troops by offering them more rewards for their service. He raised the money and land for this by further taxation and land confiscation.

 ### How did William deal with Edgar Aetheling after the rebellion of 1070?

Edgar Aetheling had a better claim to the throne than William. William countered this by paying special attention to royal ceremonies and celebrations. He made sure that he was seen in public as the king.

What happened in Ely during the rebellion of 1070?

From 1070-1071, William had to deal with the combined force of the Danes, Hereward the Wake and Earl Morcar.

- In 1070 and 1071, the Danes and Anglo-Saxon rebels raided Peterborough Abbey, and the Danes sailed away with its wealth.
- Hereward was joined by Earl Morcar, and they prepared to defend Ely.
- The Normans managed to retake Ely, possibly by bribing monks to show them the way through the marshes.
- Morcar was captured and imprisoned for life. Hereward escaped and was never heard of again.

THE EARLS' REVOLT, 1075

In 1075, William faced a different kind of rebellion. This time it was his Norman lords who rebelled.

 ### What was the Earls' Revolt?

In 1075, William faced another rebellion *(p.35)*. This time, however, the rebels were his own men - the Normans.

When was the Earls' Revolt?

The Earls' Revolt *(p.35)* occurred in 1075.

What were the aims of the Earls' Revolt?

The leaders of the Earls' Revolt *(p.35)* planned to overthrow William and divide England into three parts, shared between them.

Who was involved in the Earls' Revolt?

There were three main figures in the Earls' Revolt *(p.35)*, along with other supporters.

- ☑ Ralph de Gael, Earl of East Anglia - a Norman.
- ☑ Roger de Breteuil, Earl of Hereford - a Norman.
- ☑ Waltheof, Earl of Northumbria - an Anglo-Saxon.
- ☑ A fleet of Danish invaders, led by Sweyn's son Cnut, was assembled to help the rebels.
- ☑ Brittany and France, rivals of Normandy, were both prepared to help the earls in the revolt *(p.35)*.

What were the causes of the Earls' Revolt?

The earls are believed to have had a number of reasons for rebelling.

- ☑ They resented the loss of their lands, privileges and power.
- ☑ William was away in Normandy at the time, leaving Archbishop Lanfranc in charge.
- ☑ They had powerful allies in the form of the Danes, the French and the Bretons.
- ☑ They believed that the Anglo-Saxons were prepared to rebel.

Why did Ralph de Gael lead the Earls' Revolt?

Not much is known about Ralph de Gael's motives in rebelling against William, but it is likely that he resented having less wealth and power than his father had possessed. He also had strong links to Brittany.

Why did Roger de Breteuil lead the Earls' Revolt?

Roger de Breteuil was the son of William's most trusted advisor, but he was angry when William reduced his land in the Marcher earldom *(p.33)* and introduced his own sheriffs to the area.

Why did Earl Waltheof lead the Earls' Revolt?

Waltheof was invited to join the rebellion *(p.35)* at the wedding of de Gael to de Breteuil's sister, Emma. He was a former rebel with links to Denmark. However, he may have been a double agent in the revolt.

How did the Earls' Revolt begin?

The revolt *(p.35)* began when the rebels began to strengthen the defences of the castles in Hereford and East Anglia, and built up their troops ready to march.

Why was the wedding important in Earls' Revolt?

The wedding symbolised unity between de Gael and de Breteuil's families. It was attended by many important members of the aristocracy, and was where Waltheof was invited to join the plot.

What problems did the leaders face in the Earls' Revolt?

The leaders of the Earls' Revolt *(p.35)* faced a number of problems.

- ☑ The Anglo-Saxons did not support them.

- Waltheof changed his mind and informed Archbishop Lanfranc, who sent men to East Anglia and Hereford to find out what was going on.
- Bishop Wulfstan of Worcester and the abbot of Evesham used their troops to prevent de Breteuil from leaving Herefordshire, while de Gael was blocked in East Anglia.
- William returned to England.
- The Danish fleet of 200 ships arrived too late to help the rebels. Instead of facing William in battle, Cnut raided the east coast and then returned home.

What did Lanfranc do in the Earls' Revolt?

Archbishop Lanfranc, who had been left in charge of England while William was away, took several actions during the Earl's Revolt *(p.35)*.

- He sent men to East Anglia and Hereford to report on the rebels' actions.
- He wrote to Roger de Breteuil to remind him of his loyalty to William.
- He excommunicated de Breteuil when he didn't stop the revolt *(p.35)*.
- He made preparations to prevent the revolt *(p.35)*.

How did William react to the Earls' Revolt?

William responded severely to the Earl's revolt *(p.35)*.

- He tricked Waltheof into returning to England after he fled abroad, then imprisoned and executed him, despite his role in informing on the rebels.
- He had de Gael's Breton supporters blinded or banished, but allowed Emma safe passage to Brittany after she took refuge in Norwich castle.
- He imprisoned Roger de Breteuil for life.
- He attacked de Gael's castle in Brittany, but was forced to retreat after France sent troops to help Ralph.

What was the importance of the Earls' Revolt?

The Earls' Revolt *(p.35)* was significant for William and England in a number of ways:

- It showed that, having conquered England, William now had to watch his own supporters for treachery.
- Anglo-Saxons, such as Bishop Wulfstan, supported William rather than the rebels.
- William had Waltheof executed after the rebellion *(p.35)*, which showed that he was still ruthless about Anglo-Saxon rebellion.
- The failure of Cnut's Danish invasion marked the end of the Danish attacks on England. At the time, however, William saw it as a serious threat.

DID YOU KNOW?

Archbishop Lanfranc lived in Croydon!
In 1931, the Archbishop Lanfranc Academy was opened in Croydon, where the archbishop lived.

WILLIAM THE CONQUEROR

William duke of Normandy became William I of England. He was also known as William the Conqueror.

Who was William the Conqueror?

William was the Duke of Normandy, and became King of England after the Battle of Hastings *(p.28)* in 1066. By the time William conquered England, he had survived numerous assassination attempts as a boy and had years of military experience.

Why did William I think he should be king?

There were a number of reasons why William felt he had a strong claim to the throne.

☑ He was related to Edward the Confessor through his great-aunt, Emma of Normandy, who was Edward's mother.

☑ Before becoming king, Edward had spent over twenty years in exile in Normandy. So there was an established relationship between them.

☑ William had helped Edward in 1051, when Earl Godwin rebelled. William claimed that, in return, Edward had promised him the throne.

☑ William was an experienced ruler, and an experienced and successful warrior.

☑ William claimed that Harold Godwinson had sworn an oath to support his claim, in 1064.

What were the weaknesses of William I's claim to the throne?

Although William felt he had a strong claim to the throne, there were arguments against it.

☑ William's blood relationship to Edward was not strong.

☑ Many of the Saxons disliked the idea of a foreign king. They had objected to the number of Normans that Edward had invited to England in the 1050s.

☑ Edward had nominated Harold Godwinson on his deathbed, and the Saxons believed that deathbed promises held more weight than earlier promises.

☑ Although Harold Godwinson did not deny swearing an oath to William in 1064, he denied that he had sworn the oath to support William's claim.

How effective was William I's leadership in the Battle of Hastings?

Although the outcome of the Battle of Hastings *(p.28)* was partly determined by luck, William's leadership made the Norman chances of victory stronger. His strengths included discipline, timing, preparation, brutality, and intelligence.

How did William I use discipline at the Battle of Hastings?

William demonstrated a good ability to discipline his troops before and during the Battle of Hastings *(p.28)*.

☑ William had to keep his army and fleet ready and waiting on the French coast for the entire summer.

☑ The Norman troops did not loot or steal food from the surrounding Norman countryside during the long summer.

Did William I time his attack on England well?

William knew that eventually Harold Godwinson would have to disband the fyrd to gather the harvest. He prepared to sail as soon as he heard that this had happened, and caught Harold unawares.

How much preparation did William I make for the invasion of England?

William demonstrated thorough preparation for the invasion of England in a number of ways.

☑ The Normans took pieces of a castle over the Channel with them, and used it to transform an old Iron Age fort in Hastings into a simple defence.

- William organised for the transport of the Norman destriers using flat-bottomed ships, as the Norman horses had been especially bred for battle.
- William had excellent information from his spies, who told him what Harold was doing in England, and allowed him to meet the Anglo-Saxons at Hastings.

Were William I's troops brutal to the Anglo-Saxons in 1066?

Although the Norman troops had been well-disciplined in Normandy, William allowed them to loot and destroy English villages. This tactic enraged Harold and encouraged him to leave London.

What were William I's tactics in the Battle of Hastings?

Because he had different types of soldiers, William was able to employ a variety of tactics in the Battle of Hastings *(p.28)*.

- Feigning retreat.
- Using a combination of infantry, archers and cavalry.

Why did William I have an advantage at the Battle of Hastings?

Although Harold held the top of the hill, with his shield wall in a strong defensive position, William was able to make use of some tactical advantages. These included:

- Soldiers with a variety of fighting styles.
- His cavalry.
- Archers.
- Well-disciplined troops.

When was William I crowned king of England?

William was crowned in Westminster Abbey by Archbishop Ealdred of York, on Christmas Day 1066.

What powers did William I have?

As the first Norman king of England, William had economic, legal, military, social and religious powers.

- He controlled coins and the currency.
- He made all the laws.
- He could raise taxes - this was called 'levying the geld'.
- He owned all the land, and could grant it and take it away.
- He had military power, made up of knights provided by the tenants-in-chief.
- He could appoint important churchmen.
- He would call a meeting of the Witan to advise him.
- He issued laws and instructions by using royal writs.
- He held oath-taking ceremonies to gain the loyalty of his landholders.
- He wore the crown to show his power and position to the people.

How did William I's military power help him?

William was a strong, skilful and ruthless military leader, and this helped him to claim the crown in England.

- He was able to win the Battle of Hastings *(p.28)* and crush rebellions.
- It won the respect of the Anglo-Saxons, who admired great warriors. Many joined his side against the rebels.
- People at the time believed that his victories were a sign that he was favoured by God.

How did William I prove his legitimacy as king?

It was important to William that the Anglo-Saxons saw him as the rightful - or legitimate - king.

- ☑ He stressed that he was the rightful heir to Edward the Confessor's throne because Edward had promised it to him, because he was related to Edward, and because Harold had broken his oath.
- ☑ At his coronation he promised to uphold Edward's laws, and protect the Church.
- ☑ He made sure that he was seen wearing the crown in public at least three times a year. These included at religious festivals and in important places.
- ☑ He was crowned by Ealdred, the Archbishop of York. Normally the Archbishop of Canterbury crowned the king, but Archbishop Stigand was corrupt, and therefore was not considered appropriate.
- ☑ He made sure that images of his portrait were put onto coins so that everyone could see he was the king.

How did William I use ceremonies to show his power?

William made sure that he appeared as the true and rightful king, wearing his crown at important times and places.

- ☑ At important religious festivals, such as Christmas and Easter.
- ☑ At important places in England, such as Westminster and Gloucester.
- ☑ He also wore his crown after putting down Edgar Aetheling's rebellion (p.35) in 1069, in the ruins of York.

How did William I control money?

William took control of the minting of coins, which had his portrait on them.

How did royal writs give William I power?

Royal writs were official documents and proclamations from the king, affixed with his seal. William used them to spread his commands across the country. To begin with he issued writs in English, to show continuity from Edward's reign.

How did William I travel to maintain his power?

William travelled England frequently with his court and met with officials and important families. It made him more familiar to the people and allowed him to see what was happening throughout his kingdom.

Why did the land make William I powerful?

Owning land directly made William more powerful, as it meant that everyone ultimately relied on loyalty to him to keep their land. The link between king and landholding was much stronger than in Anglo-Saxon times.

How did oath-taking increase William I's power?

Oath-taking was making a solemn promise, and was taken very seriously by the Anglo-Saxons. William held huge oath-taking ceremonies in which men would swear to serve him faithfully.

What sort of person was William I?

William's personality seems full of contradictions, but this may have been the effect of his reputation as the conqueror and ruler of England.

- ☑ He was clearly tough and determined.
- ☑ He was the illegitimate son of Robert, duke of Normandy, and survived many assassination attempts while a boy.
- ☑ He was warlike and ruthless, showing excellent leadership and strategy.
- ☑ He was very religious, and apparently repented on his deathbed the violence he had caused.
- ☑ He focused very strongly on being accepted as the legitimate heir of Edward the Confessor, rather than merely an invader in England.

☑ He loved his wife Matilda very much, and wept for days when she died in 1083.

How many children did William I have?
William and Matilda had at least nine children.

What was William I's relationship with his children?
William had a difficult relationship with his eldest son, Robert, partly because Robert wanted more power than William was prepared to give him.

When did William I die?
William died in 1087.

☑ In July 1087, William led a raid in France but was thrown from the saddle of his horse. By this time he was very fat, and it caused serious internal injuries.

☑ He died after several weeks of suffering.

☑ On his death, the nobility fled to secure their castles from attack while the servants stole everything they could.

What happened at William I's funeral?
At William's funeral his servants tried to squeeze his body into a stone tomb, but it burst and smelled so bad everyone had to leave the cathedral. This was seen as a bad omen, indicating God's anger against him.

Who succeeded William I?
Because William was on his death-bed for a while, he had time to decide who should take the throne after him.

☑ He decided that his eldest son, Robert, should inherit the dukedom of Normandy.

☑ He wanted his favourite son, William Rufus, to be king of England, but decided to leave it in the hands of God.

☑ William Rufus left for England before his father died, with a letter from William to Lanfranc. Lanfranc crowned him William II in September 1087.

DID YOU KNOW?

You might be related to William The Conqueror!

According to some genealogists, more than 14 million English people are distantly related to him

---

BISHOP ODO OF BAYEUX
Bishop Odo of Bayeux was William's half-brother, and played an important role in England.

Who was Bishop Odo?
Bishop Odo was William's half-brother, and was awarded the earldom of Kent in England, as well as a number of other large estates.

What was Odo's relationship with William like?
Odo and William had the same mother, and probably grew up together. He lent 100 ships to William's invasion fleet and fought at the Battle of Hastings *(p.28)*.

How did Odo behave in England?

With William FitzOsbern, Odo was William's regent when he returned to Normandy in 1067. He was very powerful, unpopular with the Anglo-Saxons, and seems to have settled land disputes by himself. He was accused of making land-grabs.

Why did Odo get into trouble?

From 1076, it seems that William was less tolerant of Odo's behaviour.

- ☑ Archbishop Lanfranc took the Church's complaints against Odo to William, and in 1076 Odo was forced to hand back the land he had taken.
- ☑ In 1079, William sent Odo to Northumbria after attacks by the Scottish. Odo reportedly devastated Durham and ransacked the cathedral. He also robbed and extorted people.

Why was Odo sent to prison?

In 1082, Odo was imprisoned by William due to his greed and was not released until the king was on his deathbed.

How did Bishop Odo react to William Rufus?

Bishop Odo, freed from prison in 1087, joined the rebellion *(p.35)* to support Robert's claim as king. This may have been because he thought that Robert would be easier to control.

- ☑ Odo's brother, Robert of Mortain, also joined the rebellion. *(p.35)*
- ☑ Odo and his brother controlled large areas of the south of England.
- ☑ Odo and Robert of Mortain took refuge in Pevensey Castle, where William Rufus besieged them for six weeks.
- ☑ Both William Rufus' uncles were captured, but Odo managed to escape to Rochester Castle.
- ☑ He waited for help from his nephew, Robert, but it never came. Odo was eventually forced out of the castle by hunger and disease and was exiled.

DID YOU KNOW?

Facts about Odo of Bayeux.

- ✓ Even though he was a bishop, Odo fought at the Battle of Hastings.
- ✓ Odo is thought to have commissioned the famous Bayeux Tapestry, which tells the story of the Battle of Hastings.

WILLIAM RUFUS

When William died, he made his second son his successor. He became William II, but is usually known as William Rufus.

Who was William Rufus?

William II was known as William Rufus, possibly because of either his rosy cheeks or red hair. He faced serious challenges when he became king. William Rufus was the second of William the Conqueror's sons, and became King William II on his father's death.

What happened after William Rufus took power?

After his coronation, William Rufus faced uprisings by those who supported his brother, Robert Curthose. These included his uncle, Bishop Odo.

 ## Why was William Rufus challenged as king?

There were a number of reasons William Rufus's reign was challenged:

- ☑ William's decision before his death seemed unclear and was open to interpretation.
- ☑ Robert Curthose was made Duke of Normandy. Lords with land in both England and Normandy didn't want to answer to two different rulers.
- ☑ Robert Curthose believed he should rule England, as he was William's eldest son.

 ## How did Robert react to William Rufus' coronation?

William Rufus' brother, Robert Curthose, Duke of Normandy, also wanted to rule England and supported those who rebelled against Rufus.

 ## What other revolts did William Rufus face?

As well as those by Odo and Robert, William Rufus had to deal with smaller rebellions.

- ☑ Raids in Somerset and Wiltshire by Robert de Mowbray.
- ☑ A revolt (p.35) led by Roger Bigod in Norwich and the sheriff of Leicester.
- ☑ Raids in Gloucester by William of Eu.
- ☑ Rebellions in the west led by the Marcher earls Robert de Montgomery and Roger de Lacy.

 ## How did William Rufus win?

William Rufus used a number of effective tactics to overcome the rebellions.

- ☑ He raised an army, but took the money their lords had given the knights to live on and sent the soldiers home.
- ☑ He then used the money to bribe barons in eastern Normandy, forcing Robert to agree to rule it alongside him.
- ☑ He promised to lower taxes, to end the forest laws, and to return to Edward the Confessor's laws. This removed the complaints behind the rebellions. However, Rufus did not deliver any of these promises.

 ## Who succeeded William Rufus?

When William Rufus was killed in 1100 his youngest brother, Henry, became king.

ROBERT CURTHOSE

William, duke of Normandy became William I of England. He was also known as William the Conqueror.

 ## Who was Robert Curthose?

William's eldest son Robert was known as Robert Curthose, meaning 'short trousers'. This unflattering nickname was given to him in childhood, possibly by William. He had a number of disagreements with his father and tried to take the crown of England from his brother, William Rufus.

Why did Robert Curthose argue with William I?

Robert Curthose spent the years 1077 to 1080 effectively at war with his father. This was because he wanted more power than William was prepared to give him.

- ☑ In 1077, Robert and his army tried to take control of Rouen Castle after Robert's brothers played a prank on him and he felt William didn't punish them harshly enough.

- ☑ Robert fled to Flanders and was given a castle on Normandy's borders by the King of France. Robert launched raids against his father's land.

- ☑ William raised an army against him, but Matilda secretly sent him money, which caused a huge argument between them.

- ☑ They fought each other in battle in 1079. Robert knocked William off his horse, then gave him his own horse and ordered him to retreat. William was humiliated.

- ☑ Matilda organised a meeting between them in 1080. William made Robert the heir to Normandy again.

Why did Robert Curthose rebel against his brother?

Robert became Duke of Normandy when William the Conqueror died, but he wanted the throne of England which had gone to his brother, William Rufus.

- ☑ Norman custom generally stated that the eldest son inherited all his father's estates.

- ☑ Many Norman lords owned land in England and Normandy, and would have preferred a single ruler over both.

- ☑ His uncle, Bishop Odo, stirred up rebellion (p.35) on behalf of his claim, but Robert did not come to help him when he was besieged in Rochester Castle.

DID YOU KNOW?

Three facts about Robert of Normandy

- ✔ Robert took part in the First Crusade in the 1090s, although he left before the Crusaders reached Jerusalem in 1099.

- ✔ Robert was imprisoned for 27 years. He was 83 years old when he died in 1134.

- ✔ Robert's son, William Clito, still argued that he had a claim to the throne until he died in 1128. He was only 25 years old.

THE ACCESSION OF HENRY I

William's youngest son, Henry, eventually became king of England in 1100.

Who was Henry I.

William Rufus died in August 1100, and was succeeded by his brother, Henry. Henry was the youngest son of William the Conqueror.

When did Henry I become king?

He became king of England in 1100, and was also duke of Normandy from 1107.

How did Henry I become king?

Although Robert Curthose was Henry's older brother, Henry was in England already. He quickly took control and had himself crowned king.

How did Henry I gain control in England and Normandy?

Robert Curthose still wanted to be king of England as well as duke of Normandy. However, Henry was able to consolidate his power.

- ☑ In 1101, Henry and Robert reached an agreement, in which they would each stay in their own territory.
- ☑ However, Henry attacked Normandy, and defeated his brother at the Battle of Tinchebrai in 1106.
- ☑ By 1107, Henry was the ruler of England and Normandy and the two lands were united again.
- ☑ Henry put his brother Robert in prison, where he remained for the rest of his life.

DID YOU KNOW?

Three facts about Henry I

- ✔ Henry was known as 'Beauclerc', which indicated that he was well educated and interested in reading.
- ✔ Henry had over 20 children - but only two of them were legitimate.
- ✔ His only legitimate son drowned at the age of 20. Henry then nominated his daughter to succeed him - which led to a 19-year civil war in England.

THE NORMANS AND LAND

After his victory at Hastings, William now 'owned' the whole of England. He set about transferring the land from the remaining Saxon lords to his own, Norman followers.

? What happened to land under the Normans?

From 1066 until his death in 1087, William I oversaw the transfer of land from Anglo-Saxon to Norman ownership. This formed the basis of the feudal system *(p.54)*.

 Why was land important for the Normans?

Land ownership provided food, money, followers and fighting men. It was therefore a source of power in England during William's reign.

 What changed for the Normans about land-owning during William I's reign?

By the end of William's reign, much of the land in England had been redistributed to Normans, rather than Anglo-Saxons. Large portions were owned by the king and the Church, and estates were consolidated.

- ☑ The land had been redistributed to Normans, rather than Anglo-Saxons.
- ☑ Large portions were owned by the Church, which was controlled in England by the Normans.
- ☑ The king directly owned about one fifth of the land.
- ☑ Estates were consolidated, and a small number of lords held large amounts of land.

 How much land did the Church own in Norman England?

A quarter of the land was owned by the Church, but the Normans held all the important Church positions.

 Who had the most land in Norman England?

Although William was careful not to allow any individual more power than he had himself, he did consolidate land ownership among fewer people.

- By 1087, over half the land in England was held by around 190 tenants-in-chief. Of these, only two were Anglo-Saxons.
- Half the land held by the tenants-in-chief was held by 11 men. These included William's greatest supporters, such as Odo and William FitzOsbern.

How much land did the Anglo-Saxons get in Norman England?

By 1087, less than 5% of the land was held by Anglo-Saxons, and this was mostly in the form of smaller estates.

What happened to the thegns' land in Norman England?

There were about 4,000 thegns holding land in England when William took over in 1066. These were a potential threat to his rule.

- William took land from the thegns. By 1086 only four Anglo-Saxon thegns remained.
- Thegns were dependant on the Normans for the small amounts of land that they still held.
- The thegns' way of life was destroyed. Many went to Europe as mercenaries.

Why did William I change land-ownership in Norman England?

William had some good reasons for changing land-ownership in England after 1066.

- The rebellions of 1068-1071 showed that the Anglo-Saxons couldn't be trusted.
- He didn't want any one individual to have enough land to challenge his power.
- He had promised his followers land and riches if they fought for him at Hastings. He had to make good on that promise.

How was the land redistributed in Norman England?

The Normans used three main methods to transfer land-ownership from Anglo-Saxons to Normans.

- By forfeit. The king, who owned all land, could confiscate land taken from the disloyal and give it to new lords of his choice.
- New earldoms were made up of land that had belonged to other landholders, particularly to defend areas where there was unrest, such as the Welsh marches.
- Sometimes the Normans snatched land from Anglo-Saxons, through corrupt dealings or just by taking it. These land-grabs were illegal.

Which parts of English land did William I give to the Normans?

William was able to use his conquest and the rebellions to redistribute lands.

- After the Battle of Hastings *(p.28)*, William gave the Godwinson lands in the south and west of England to his followers.
- After the rebellions of 1068-1071, he redistributed the land in Mercia, Northumbria and East Anglia.

How did William I take control of the land in Norman England?

After 1071 William changed some of his lords' grants of land, so that they held more of it in the same place.

- Before 1071, forfeited Anglo-Saxon land was passed to the Norman lords in bits and pieces, which meant they often held land in different regions.
- After 1071, William consolidated more blocks of land. This meant that there was a single authority in an area and wa better for control.
- Before 1071, William had claimed that he was maintaining Anglo-Saxon traditions, but afterwards he took a more pragmatic approach to keep control.

CHANGES TO LANDHOLDING UNDER THE NORMANS

The main features of landholding in Norman England.

How did landholding change under the Normans?

The Normans introduced changes to landholding, including the way that land could be given out, the duties associated with holding it, and how secure and reliable it was.

How did landholding work under the Anglo-Saxons before the Normans changed them?

There were different types of tenure under the Anglo-Saxons.

- ☑ Bookland was when the lords granted the right to land to their followers, which was represented by a charter. This could be passed on to heirs or sold.
- ☑ Leases were when land was loaned to someone in return for money for a set amount of time.
- ☑ All landowners had to provide one fyrdman for every five hides, and pay geld tax.
- ☑ A tax was due to the lord when a new landholder inherited land from a dead one.

How did William I change landholding in Norman England?

There were some similarities, but some significant differences to landholding under the Normans.

- ☑ The king owned all the land, and this over-rode any previous agreements.
- ☑ Anglo-Saxons had to pay William money for the right to carry on using their land.
- ☑ Land granted by William to his followers did not need money to redeem. However, if they died without an heir then the land went back to the king. Any heirs had to pay a 'relief' (tax) to the king on inheriting their land.

Why did William change landholding in Norman England?

William had a number of reasons for changing methods of landholding in England.

- ☑ It gave him more control. Anyone who disobeyed him could be left without land.
- ☑ It earned him money, through the relief paid to redeem and inherit land.
- ☑ It made tenure less safe, which meant that tenants were more dependent on their lords and therefore less likely to rebel.

How much power did the tenants-in-chief have over landholding in Norman England?

The tenants-in-chief were extremely powerful in Norman England, and had firm control over land ownership in their areas.

- ☑ They became the lords of the thegns in the area.

- ☑ They could reallocate land if a thegn died.
- ☑ They could make their supporters 'heirs' to a thegn's land.
- ☑ They could take land away from anyone who acted against them.

 How did landholding change things for the peasants in Norman England?

There were fewer ceorls (freemen) in Norman England, as the Norman lords increased rents which they could not afford. Many freemen therefore became un-free villeins.

THE FEUDAL SYSTEM

The social hierarchy of England was established through landholding, in what has become known as the 'feudal system'.

 What was the feudal system?

The feudal system is the name given to the way Norman society was structured.

 What was the hierarchy of the feudal system?

The feudal system was a hierarchy of four main classes, or groups.

- ☑ The king was at the top of the system.
- ☑ Tenants-in-chief, important landholding lords, were less important than the king but more powerful than the under-tenants.
- ☑ Vassals, or under-tenants, who were often knights, were less important than the tenants-in-chief but more powerful than the peasants.
- ☑ Peasants were the lowest class in Norman society.

 What did the king do in the feudal system?

The king had ultimate power in the feudal system. He owned all the land, and demanded loyalty from everyone who received it.

 What did the tenants-in-chief do in the feudal system?

The tenants-in-chief received large areas of land from the king. In return, they promised to provide him with troops when they were needed. Land that was given under these circumstances was called a fief.

 What did the vassals do in the feudal system?

The under-tenants, or vassals, received areas of land from the tenants-in-chief. In return, they gave military service to the tenants-in-chief.

 What did the peasants do in the feudal system?

The peasants received small strips of land from their lords, which they farmed for themselves. In return, they had to do boon work' on the lord's land for some days of the week.

 What about slaves in the feudal system in Norman England?

The Normans thought that slavery was wrong and gradually ended the practice in England.

What role did the Church have in the feudal system?

The Church played an important role in the feudal system.

- ✅ It was a major landholder and owned up to 25% of English land. Church tenants did boon work for the church, and the church collected the taxes for the king.
- ✅ Bishops owed the king military service, so the Church gave land to knights and made sure it could provide soldiers when needed.
- ✅ Bishops were the head of cathedrals and the area around them, known as the diocese. They helped to enforce the king's laws.
- ✅ Royal clerks were recruited from the Church to write legal documents, and important churchmen sometimes acted as judges.

DID YOU KNOW?

The Normans did not introduce the feudal system to England: it already existed in Saxon times. But the Normans adapted and developed it for their own purposes.

EXCHANGES IN THE FEUDAL SYSTEM

The feudal system worked on the basis of duties and obligations, by the king or lord as well as their tenants.

What was exchanged in the feudal system?

The feudal system *(p.54)* was a system of exchange of land, loyalty and labour.

How was land exchanged in the feudal system?

In the feudal system *(p.54)*, all of the land belonged to the king. This made his life simpler in a number of ways.

- ✅ Nobody could inherit land without making a relief payment to the king and swearing an oath of homage.
- ✅ The system of paying a relief encouraged loyalty to the king and also raised money for him.
- ✅ The king could reward favourites with low relief payments for their sons, and use high relief payments as a threat for rebellious ones.
- ✅ This system prevented any noble from gaining so much land that they could challenge the king.

How was homage exchanged in the feudal system?

The ceremony of homage was an important event in which the tenant-in-chief *(p.56)* knelt before the king and said 'I become your man'. He then swore on the Bible to remain loyal to the king for the rest of his life.

How was labour exchanged in the feudal system?

Peasants promised to work for their lord in return for enough land to support themselves.

- ✅ Sometimes this meant working on the lord's land to plough, sow and gather crops. This was known as 'boon work'.
- ✅ Sometimes this meant giving a set amount of their produce to the lord each year, as a form of tax.
- ✅ Peasants in towns had to do labour service for any land they farmed outside the town *(p.67)*.

TENANTS-IN-CHIEF

William's rule in England was supported by his tenants-in-chief, the great lords of the kingdom.

What were tenants in chief?

The tenants-in-chief were directly answerable to the king, and played an important role in Norman society. They were large landholders, who received their land directly from the Norman king.

What was the military role of the tenants-in-chief?

Tenants-in-chief had to lead their own army to fight with the king. They were also expected to defend their own land and put down any rebellions there.

How did the tenants-in-chief use their land?

It was up to tenants-in-chief how they used their land to raise an army. With huge fiefdoms, they were integral to the system of land distribution.

How did tenants-in-chief run their fiefs?

A collection of fiefdoms belonging to a tenant-in-chief was called a barony, and each had its own court to sort out disputes.

What role did tenants-in-chief play in the economy?

Tenants-in-chief were very wealthy, even though they passed on some of their revenues to the king.

What political role did the tenants-in-chief play?

Tenants-in-chief sat on the king's council and might give him advice. They also hosted the king and his court when he travelled to their area.

DID YOU KNOW?

The earl of Arundel is one of the oldest noble titles in England. The first earl was created in 1138, and the title is currently held by the duke of Norfolk, who still sits in the House of Lords.

KNIGHTS

Norman power relied on military force, which was represented by the knights.

What were knights in Norman England?

There were an estimated 6,000 knights in Norman England, and they were an important part of the military system in the country.

What was the status of knights in Norman England?

Knights had varying status.

- ☑ Some were granted very little land, or might be retained by a lord as a 'household' knight.
- ☑ Knights replaced thegns as the under-tenants to the tenants-in-chief.

Quizzes, amazing exam preparation tools and more at GCSEHistory.com

- ☑ Many knights were the local lords of the manor.
- ☑ They held manor courts to try small disputes among their tenants.

What was the role of knights in Norman England?

Knights had a number of duties in Norman society:

- ☑ They were expected to guard the lord's property.
- ☑ They had to provide 40 days' military service to the king. This could be to fight in a war, or to garrison a castle in peacetime.
- ☑ Rich or powerful knights fought for the king.

What skills did knights have in Norman England?

Knights were extremely well-trained and equipped. They trained as cavalrymen from a very young age.

How were knights used for defence in Norman England?

William needed knights for the defence of England:

- ☑ Against the Vikings.
- ☑ For wars in Wales and Scotland.
- ☑ For wars in France.
- ☑ To put down rebellions.
- ☑ To garrison castles in order to control the local population.

DID YOU KNOW?

The word 'knight' did not always mean a mounted warrior.

- ✔ The word knight comes from the Old English word 'cniht', which originally meant 'boy'.
- ✔ The French word for knight is 'chevalier', meaning someone who rides a horse. From this we get the English word 'cavalier'.

FORFEITURE

As well as gaining great benefit from the feudal system, the lords of England had to be kept in check by the threat of losing their land.

What was forfeiture?

If anyone failed to obey their lord, or did not provide the taxes or services they owed, they could be punished with the loss of their land. This was called forfeiture. For peasants it often meant that they became un-free villeins.

CHANGES TO ENGLAND UNDER THE NORMANS

An overview of the main changes that the Normans brought to England.

How much did the Normans change England?

After William conquered England, the Normans kept some things the same, but introduced important changes to English society.

What did the Normans change in England?

The Normans changed a number of important aspects of life in England.

- ☑ Government.
- ☑ Law Enforcement.
- ☑ The use of land and the new forests.
- ☑ Taxes and the Domesday Book *(p.64)*.
- ☑ The Church.

NORMAN GOVERNMENT

Norman government was a sophisticated regime. William continued with many of the Saxon features of government, as well as introducing some key changes.

What was William's government like in Norman England?

William's government showed a lot of continuity with the Anglo-Saxon government, but he also took opportunities to centralise his power.

What did William keep the same in the Norman government?

William kept a number of important features of Anglo-Saxon government when he took over England.

- ☑ The Anglo-Saxon government was much more sophisticated than the government in Normandy, so William kept many aspects of it when he took over England.
- ☑ The Norman government used the land divisions of 'hides' to work out taxes.
- ☑ They kept the land divisions of shires and hundreds.
- ☑ William still consulted the Witan, or a similar royal council.
- ☑ The Normans still used the silver pennies used by the Anglo-Saxons.
- ☑ The royal treasury remained at Winchester.

How did William limit the power of earls in Norman government?

Edward the Confessor had experienced numerous problems because of the power held by earls such as Godwin. William took the opportunity to limit how much power they could gain.

- ☑ When his loyal followers were replaced, William made their earldoms smaller or, like Wessex and Mercia, redistributed them altogether.
- ☑ The special powers given to the Marcher earls immediately after the invasion were gradually reduced.
- ☑ Earls were tenants-in-chief, and could be punished by forfeiture like other tenants.

How did William use regents in the Norman government?

William had two countries to run, and therefore was absent from either for periods of time. While he was away he appointed regents to keep control in his absence.

- ☑ William's first two regents, Bishop Odo and William FitzOsbern, caused problems and resentment among the Anglo-Saxons in 1067.
- ☑ Archbishop Lanfranc was William's regent in 1075, and helped to prevent the Earls' Revolt *(p.35)*.
- ☑ William often left his wife, Matilda, as regent of Normandy.
- ☑ He tended to return quickly when he heard of problems in England.

DID YOU KNOW?

The way the British government works today has its roots in the Norman system of government. Many aspects of the British Parliament still use words derived from Norman-French.

THE NORMAN SHERIFF

The role of the sheriff in local government in Norman England.

What was a sheriff in Norman England?

The sheriff was the name given to the law enforcement officer who had been known by the Anglo-Saxons as the shire reeve.

What was the job of the sheriff?

William kept the role of the sheriff relatively similar after he took power in England. This role involved:

- ☑ Acting as the king's representative, collecting taxes and looking after the king's personal estates.
- ☑ He administered justice and made sure that the shire met its military obligations.

How did the sheriff's role stay the same?

William kept the sheriff's role more or less the same as it had been in Anglo-Saxon times. However, he replaced the Anglo-Saxons sheriffs with Normans by 1071.

- ☑ Sheriffs were still appointed by the king.
- ☑ The Normans kept the same legal system, with some new punishments for rebellion. *(p.35)*
- ☑ Norman sheriffs continued organising the defence of the shire and gathering men for military service.

How did the sheriff's role change under William?

Some aspects of the sheriff's role changed under William.

- ☑ They were entitled to a share of the taxes that they collected, and could keep the money paid in fines in the shire courts.
- ☑ Sheriffs paid a set sum to the king to collect taxes. Anything they collected above that sum counted as profit.
- ☑ Unlike in Anglo-Saxon times, the sheriff had greater power than the earl in his shire, as he answered directly to the king. Some sheriffs were very powerful and important.
- ☑ Norman sheriffs lost some control when the Church set up its own courts for churchmen in 1076.
- ☑ As well as organising the fyrd, sheriffs were also responsible for overseeing knight *(p.56)* service.

☑ Sheriffs were often responsible for the king's castles in the shire.

Why were sheriffs unpopular in Norman England?

Many sheriffs became very unpopular with the Anglo-Saxons. The new Norman laws made it profitable for them to raise taxes for themselves, and they were often involved in land-grabs.

THE NORMAN LEGAL SYSTEM

Law and order was a key feature of government. William kept many features of the Saxon legal system, but introduced some key changes.

 What was the Norman legal system?

One of the main features of Norman government was the legal system. William I kept most of the Saxon system, but did introduce some important changes.

 How did Norman law enforcement work?

The Normans kept the Anglo-Saxon system of local community law enforcement and collective responsibility, with trials by ordeal run by the Church.

 What stayed the same in the Norman legal system?

When William became king he promised to keep the laws of Edward the Confessor. He did this for various reasons.

☑ The Saxon legal system was sophisticated and it worked. There was no need to change it.

☑ Keeping Saxon laws meant continuity and would help William's claim to be the legitimate king of England.

☑ Keeping Saxon laws removed a reason for the Saxon population to rebel against Norman rule.

 How did the Normans change the legal system?

Although he kept much of the Saxon legal system in place, William did make a few important changes.

☑ He introduced some new laws, in order to maintain Norman power in England.

☑ He introduced new courts, which increased the power of Norman lords over their lands.

☑ He made changes to the way criminals were punished, which helped to maintain Norman power and also made money for the king.

☑ The Normans centralised the system. Under the Saxons there had been many regional variations in the laws and legal system, so the Normans introduced uniformity throughout the country.

☑ Under the Normans, the language *(p.75)* of the law became Norman-French. This was a disadvantage to the Saxons, most of whom did not speak the language.

 What new laws did the Normans introduce?

Although William I kept most of the existing Saxon laws, he did introduce some new ones to ensure the Normans kept their power and control.

☑ He introduced new laws, such as the murdrum fine, to protect his Norman followers against attacks by the Saxons.

☑ He introduced the forest laws to protect the land he set aside as his own hunting grounds.

☑ He introduced new laws on inheritance *(p.63)* to prevent his lords' estates from being broken up. This helped his lords to consolidate and maintain their power.

What was murdrum in the Norman legal system?

The murdrum fine was introduced by the Normans. If a Norman was killed, people in the local area had five days to produce the murderer. If they failed, they faced a large fine.

How did the Normans enforce the law?

The Saxon system of law enforcement, which worked on the principle of collective responsibility, was effective. The Normans continued this.

- ☑ Normans continued the Anglo-Saxon tradition of constables and watchmen who were elected or appointed in towns. They kept the peace and enforced curfews.
- ☑ The tithing was kept, where groups of men guaranteed each other's good behaviour.
- ☑ The hue and cry remained and was raised whenever a crime was committed. Everyone was expected to help chase and catch the criminal or face a fine.

How did trials work in the Norman legal system?

The Normans kept the Saxon methods of trying criminals. As evidence was sometimes difficult to produce, there were various ways to establish innocence or guilt.

- ☑ People would swear oaths in court about a person's guilt or innocence, based on their knowledge of the person. As oaths were religious rituals, people were expected to tell the truth or face God's punishment.
- ☑ Trial by ordeal (p.62) was sometimes used. The Saxon ordeals included trial by cold water and trial by hot iron. The Normans also introduced trial by combat (or trial by battle).

What were the courts in the Norman legal system?

Trials were held in the courts. The Normans kept most of the Saxon courts, but also introduced new ones.

- ☑ The King's Court dealt with royal pleas, including the most serious offences: murder, treason, arson, robbery and rape. The king would also hear appeals from the lower courts.
- ☑ The Shire Courts were supervised by the sheriff (or shire-reeve). These met regularly in each shire and made judgements on violent crime and theft. They also heard land disputes.
- ☑ The Hundred Courts were held monthly and supervised by a bailiff, who was appointed by the sheriff. These dealt with minor disputes that did not need to be heard by the sheriff himself.
- ☑ The Lord's Court (or honorial court) was introduced by the Normans. Lords could deal with their tenants, hearing criminal cases and disputes and also dealing with property transactions.
- ☑ The Manor Courts were held at village (p.66) level. Each lord of the manor would deal with cases arising from day-to-day life.
- ☑ The Normans also introduced Church Courts. These dealt with religious and moral crimes, including adultery. Church courts were also reserved to try members of the Church for any crime.

What punishments were there in the Norman legal system?

Norman punishments tended to be harsher than under Saxon kings. They also provided revenue for the king which increased his wealth.

- ☑ If the accused was found innocent, the accuser was punished for making a false claim and had to pay a fine to both the king and the accused.
- ☑ Some lesser crimes such as theft or causing injury were settled by paying compensation to the victim. This was similar to the Saxon system.
- ☑ The Saxons had operated wergild for more serious crimes, where compensation was paid to the victim's family. Every freeman had a wergild price.
- ☑ Under the Normans, wergild declined. Serious offences were now punished by hanging or mutilation. The Normans were more inclined to use brutality and terror as a deterrent.
- ☑ Fines paid for more serious offences now went to the king rather than the victim's family.

TRIALS BY ORDEAL

Trial by ordeal was a key feature of the legal process, which demonstrated the power of religion in the provision of justice.

What was trial by ordeal?

In early medieval times, when the guilt of a criminal could not be decided, a trial by ordeal was held to allow God to determine whether or not an accused was guilty.

Which trials by ordeal did the Anglo-Saxons use?

The Anglo-Saxons used 4 main trials by ordeal.

- Trial by hot water.
- Trial by hot iron, often used for women accused of crimes.
- Trial by cold water, often used for serfs or other people of low status.
- Trial by consecrated (or blessed) bread, which was taken by priests.

Which trial by ordeal did the Normans introduce?

As well as the Anglo-Saxon trials by ordeal, the Normans used trial by combat.

How was combat used in the trial by ordeal?

Trial by combat was where the accused fought with the accuser until one of them was killed or unable to fight on. The loser was then hanged, as God had judged them to be guilty.

How was hot water used in the trial of ordeal?

For a trial by hot water, the accused had to plunge their hand into boiling water and have it bandaged for three days. If the burn healed well, this was seen as a sign God judged the person to be innocent.

How was hot iron used in a trial by ordeal?

In trial by hot iron, hot iron was used to burn the hand, which was bandaged for three days. If the burn healed well, this was seen as a sign God had found the person innocent.

How was cold water used in a trial of ordeal?

In trial by cold water, the accused had their arms tied and was thrown into a pond or river that had been blessed by a priest. Those who floated were found guilty as God had 'rejected' them, while those who sank were judged innocent and hauled up again.

How was blessed bread used in a trial of ordeal?

Trial by consecrated, or blessed, bread was taken by priests. He would first have to pray, asking that he be choked by the bread if he lied. If he did, it meant he was guilty.

How were trials by ordeal conducted in Anglo-Saxon times?

There were 3 important procedures in the way the trials by ordeal were run.

- ☑ Because the trials were designed to allow God to decide on the guilt or innocence of the accused, a priest had to be present.
- ☑ The accused would often spend three days at a holy site or in a church or monastery *(p.74)* before the trial, praying and fasting.
- ☑ The accused would attend mass before the trial.

NORMAN INHERITANCE LAWS

William made major changes to the rules by which people could inherit land in England.

How did the Normans change inheritance?

The Anglo-Saxons traditionally divided the estates of a dead man amongst his sons. This meant that estates became smaller and smaller, and sometimes led to conflict between family members. The Normans changed inheritance laws.

What did the Normans change about inheritance law?

The Normans made five important changes to inheritance.

- ☑ The Normans introduced male primogeniture, where the eldest son inherited all the lands of the father. This helped to keep estates intact.
- ☑ When a man died without an heir his lands returned to the lord, who could keep it or grant it to another of his followers.
- ☑ If an heir was under-age, the lord took over the land until the heir was of age. He could enjoy the revenue of the land until that time.
- ☑ Widows came under the control of the lord or king. He could arrange a new marriage for her, often to one of his followers, who then gained the land.
- ☑ If the deceased only had daughters, they came under the control of the lord or king. He could arrange their marriage to one of his followers, who then gained the land.

DID YOU KNOW?

The Norman inheritance law of male primogeniture was used in the succession to the throne right up to 2015. It was abolished in case the first child of the Duke and Duchess of Sussex was a girl.

THE ROYAL FORESTS

*William and the rest of the Normans were keen on hunting. To satisfy his fondness for hunting,
William created the Royal Forests, with strict laws to accompany them.*

What were the Royal Forests?

William kept a bigger area of land for himself ('demesne') than Edward the Confessor had previously. He turned a lot of land into the 'Royal Forests' - land reserved for hunting.

Why did William make the Royal Forests?

William created the Royal Forests because he really enjoyed hunting, particularly deer.

How did William create the Royal Forests?

William confiscated land from other land-holders, including the church, and evicted families from their homes.

What laws covered the Royal Forests?

Numerous laws were created to protect William's hunting grounds and the animals in them.

- ✅ Hunting on private land became a new crime, known as poaching.
- ✅ Damage to the animals or vegetation was prohibited.
- ✅ It was an offence to take weapons or dogs into the forest.
- ✅ It was illegal for ordinary people to hurt the deer, even if the animals were damaging crops.

Why were the Royal Forests important?

The Royal Forests were significant in a number of ways.

- ✅ When William extended his area of land, he legitimised land-grabs being committed by other Normans and made them seem acceptable.
- ✅ It showed the power of the king was greater than the existing law.
- ✅ Harsh punishments for poaching demonstrated Norman ruthlessness.
- ✅ The Anglo-Saxon population began to resent the forests.
- ✅ The forest areas became another source of income for the king.

THE DOMESDAY BOOK

*In the 1080s, William set out to create a survey of landholding in England. This became known as
the Domesday Survey, or the Domesday Book.*

What was the Domesday Book?

The Domesday Book was a survey of England that William commissioned at the end of 1085. It aimed to find out how much was owned by each landholder, and whether they could pay more tax.

Why was the Domesday Book created?

The Domesday Book was produced because William needed to raise more taxes.

- ✅ There was a heavy geld tax in 1084.

- In 1085 William raised a massive - and expensive - army to defend England against the threat of a Viking invasion *(p.26)*.
- In 1085, while the Domesday Book was being written, William raised another tax.
- It may have been a way of getting around the special privileges that meant that many tenants-in-chief didn't have to pay tax on some of their land.

What was in the Domesday Book?

The Domesday Book was a huge document.

- The Domesday Book was a record of what each landholder owned in each area of England.
- It was 913 pages long and recorded details of about 1,000 tenants-in-chief and 8,000 under-tenants.
- It was later called the Domesday Book because the comprehensive information it gathered made people feel as if they had reached the Day of Judgement ('Doomsday').
- It was written in Latin.

What was the significance of the Domesday Book?

The Domesday Book was an important document that affected the economy, the military, and the law in Norman England.

What was the financial significance of the Domesday Book?

The Domesday Book allowed the king and his clerks to see how much money in tax, or relief payments, were owed on each estate.

What was the legal significance of the Domesday Book?

The Domesday Book was a way of sorting out legal disputes, especially for Anglo-Saxons who claimed to have lost land in land-grabs.

What was the military significance of the Domesday Book?

The Domesday Book allowed William to see how many soldiers were available if they were needed, for example in response to the Viking threat of 1085.

DID YOU KNOW?

Facts about the Domesday Survey.

- ✔ There were actually two books, and they are kept in the National Archives at Kew, in London.
- ✔ You can look up any place mentioned in the Domesday Survey online. You can find out who owned the place where you live in 1086!

THE DIFFERENCE BETWEEN A VILLAGE AND A TOWN

The majority of the population lived in rural villages, although there were towns, too. It is important to understand the difference between a village and a town.

What's the difference between a town and a village?

Villages are rural communities where the main work is farming. Towns are where non-farming activities take place - manufacturing and trade.

HOW VILLAGES CHANGED UNDER THE NORMANS

Life in a village remained largely the same under Norman rule, although there were some significant changes.

What was life like in Norman villages?

Around 95% of the population lived in villages, and the economy was mostly based on sheep farming and the growing of crops. Life was hard, and bad harvests could result in starvation.

How many villages were there in Norman England?

The Domesday Book *(p.64)*, in 1086, recorded nearly 13,500 villages in England.

- ☑ Villages varied in size, but many would only have a handful of families. A village of 67 families was large, while some only had five or six households.

- ☑ However, the Normans had destroyed large parts of the north of England in the Harrying of the North of 1069/70. One third of Yorkshire was described in 1086 as 'waste'.

Who were the peasants in Norman villages?

The peasants, who worked the land, were all Saxon. But there were different types of peasant.

- ☑ Freemen paid the lord rent for their land. Often they also carried out 'boon work' - unpaid extra work on the lord's demesne.

- ☑ Villeins were unfree peasants, who worked on the lord's land for no pay. They had a little land to farm for themselves. They could not leave the land without the lord's permission.

- ☑ Bordars and cottars were poorer villeins, who rarely had enough land of their own to live on.

- ☑ Around 10% of the population were slaves, who had no freedom and no land. The Normans gradually got rid of slavery, but it took time.

What work did peasants do in Norman villages?

Many aspects of village life did not change after the Norman Conquest. Peasants' work did not change, as it was guided by the weather and the seasons.

- ☑ Each village was surrounded by large fields, which were divided into strips. Each peasant had a few strips of land to farm.

- ☑ The villagers agreed which crops to grow in each field. Much of the year was spent ploughing, sowing seeds and growing crops, and harvesting them at the end of the summer.

- ☑ Villagers also had their own gardens, which they used to grow fruit and vegetables. They also kept chickens and other animals.

- ☑ Villages also had common land, where all the villagers grazed their animals - such as the oxen they used for ploughing.

- ☑ There was often woodland, too, where pigs could root for acorns, and where villagers collected firewood.

- All work was done by hand, apart from ploughing, which was done by ox-drawn ploughs - these were owned in common by the whole village.

What did people eat in Norman villages?

People's diets did not change after the Norman Conquest. But there was a big difference between what Saxon peasants and Norman lords ate.

- Peasants ate what they could grow. Their diet basically consisted of bread, oat porridge and vegetables. They got dairy products from the animals they kept. Eating meat was a luxury.
- By contrast, the Norman lords had much more variety. They also ate bread, but it was better quality than the peasants' bread. They ate much more meat, and fewer vegetables and dairy products. Overall, the Norman lords' diet was much worse than the peasants'.

What were houses like in Norman villages?

The houses that the Saxon peasants and the Norman lords lived in were also very different.

- Peasants lived in single-room houses, which were dark, damp and smoky. They usually did not have windows, a fire in the middle of the room was used for warmth and cooking. The peasants brought their animals into the house at night.
- The Norman lord lived in a much grander manor house. The manor house was usually built of stone. Although most business took place in the large hall, the lord had a separate sleeping chamber, and usually a separate kitchen building (p.72). The manor house had windows, although it still relied on a central hearth for heat.

Who was the bailiff in a Norman village?

The bailiff was the man in charge of making sure that the villagers did their work, especially on the lord's land. He was usually chosen from amongst the villagers.

How did villages change under the Normans?

Although village life largely stayed the same, the Normans did introduce some significant changes after 1066.

- Almost all the old Saxon lords were replaced by Norman lords, who aimed to make more money from their new lands.
- Almost every village had a church, which was built of stone. Wooden Saxon churches were pulled down and rebuilt.
- The lords also built large manor houses from stone. Again, any wooden Saxon manor houses were rebuilt.
- Many Norman lords built mills for grinding flour. The peasants had to use the lord's mill, and had to pay for the privilege.
- The Norman lords charged more rent from their freemen. Many could not afford these higher rents, so became villeins.
- The Normans did gradually end slavery, however, largely because the Church disapproved of enslaving Christians.

HOW TOWNS CHANGED UNDER THE NORMANS

Norman rule saw a growth in the number and wealth of towns in England.

How did towns change in Norman England?

There were not many towns in Saxon England. Under the Normans, the number and size of towns changed, and the towns themselves developed.

How many towns were there in Norman England?

The number and size of towns increased because the Normans had greater trade links with mainland Europe.

☑ In 1086, there were 18 towns with populations over 2,000 people. There were 112 smaller towns.

☑ London had more than 10,000 people. Winchester had more than 6,000. Norwich, York and Lincoln had populations of 4-5,000.

What did Norman towns look like?

Norman towns shared a number of basic features. Some of these were features that developed specifically under the Normans. They included the following:

☑ A market square, where most commercial business took place.

☑ A high street, which led from the gates to the market square. This was wider than the other streets. Often, Saxon houses were demolished to make space.

☑ Merchants operated their business from buildings on the high street. They used painted signs to show what goods and services they offered.

☑ Towns had churches - often more than one. Some also had monasteries or abbeys.

☑ Many towns now had castles. Saxon houses were often destroyed to make room to build *(p.72)* the castle.

☑ Towns were cramped and overcrowded. This led to a greater risk of disease, fires, and theft.

Who were the citizens of a Norman town?

Burgesses were the citizens of a town. They had to serve as watchmen, and help the town militia in times of trouble. They also had to pay taxes.

What privileges did Norman towns have?

Towns enjoyed certain privileges and legal rights, that made them very different from the villages in the countryside.

☑ Burgesses (town citizens) could only be tried in the town courts.

☑ They also enjoyed freedom of movement, unlike the villeins who served on the land.

☑ If a villein escaped from the land and managed to live in a town for a year and a day without getting caught, then he became a freeman.

What was a charter in Norman town?

If a town was granted a charter from the local lord or the king, it gained independence.

☑ The town could govern itself through a town council, and elect a mayor.

☑ The town could hold a fair or market regularly. This helped to stimulate trade and the town's economy.

☑ A charter town could set its own taxes. It still had to pay taxes to the local lord or the king, though!

What was the hierarchy in Norman towns?

Towns had a social hierarchy, just as villages did. There were people at the top, and also at the bottom of town society.

☑ At the top were merchants, lawyers, doctors, and other property owners. These men became rich during the Norman period.

☑ In the middle were craftsmen, who were skilled workers (such as smiths, barbers, apothecaries, carpenters). One they were masters they could become rich.

☑ At the bottom were unskilled workers and labourers, and the servants of the town's wealthier citizens.

What were guilds in Norman towns?

A guild was a society of merchants and craftsmen. They controlled prices and the quality of goods. They could decide who was allowed to carry out business in the town.

Quizzes, amazing exam preparation tools and more at GCSEHistory.com

What was an apprentice in a Norman town?

Apprentices were boys who signed up to learn *(p.76)* a craft or trade, so that they could eventually become a master craftsman.

- ☑ An apprentice had to work hard and for long hours. But in return he was fed, clothed and housed by his master.

Who were craftsmen in Norman towns?

Once an apprentice had served his master for seven years, he was considered to have learned his trade. He could then become a craftsman.

- ☑ At this point he became a journeyman. He could work for anyone, and he was paid daily wages for his work.
- ☑ Eventually, a craftsman could become a master. He proved his skill by producing a perfect piece of work (his 'masterpiece'). He could then set up his own business.

DID YOU KNOW?

Some towns grew around a new castle or a monastery.

One such town was Bury St Edmunds. Within the 20 years from 1066 to the Domesday Book, more than 300 houses were built on land in Bury St Edmunds that had previously been used for farming.

THE NORMANS AND CHRISTIANITY

The Normans were Christian, and deeply religious.

What was religion like in Norman times?

The Normans were Christian and very religious, but also very violent and focused on warfare. They reconciled this by doing 'penance', praying and building *(p.72)* churches to gain forgiveness for their sins.

THE NORMAN CHURCH

The Normans used the Church to help them control England. William made significant reforms to the Church in England.

What was the role of the Church in Norman society?

The Church played a key role in Norman society, and the English Church changed as a result of this.

What role did the Norman Church play in the military?

Bishops owed the king military service, so the Church gave land to knights and made sure it could provide soldiers when needed.

What role did the Norman Church play in landholding?

It was a major landholder and owned up to 25% of English land. Church tenants did land service, just as for any other lord, and the Church collected the taxes for the king.

What legal role did the Church play in Norman England?

Because churchmen were among the few literate members of the population, they had an important role to play in the legal system.

- ☑ Church clerks wrote the king's royal writs and looked after his seal.
- ☑ Bishops sometimes developed laws for the king.
- ☑ They advised the king on legal matters.
- ☑ The Church organised Trials by Ordeal, where God was given the chance to show the guilt of those accused of crimes.
- ☑ William allowed the Church to create its own courts, which dealt with church-related crimes, blasphemy, and legal cases involving marriage.

 What political role did the Church play in Norman England?

Important churchmen often paid a key role in William's government.

- ☑ Bishops and abbots often acted as William's advisers.
- ☑ They sometimes acted as the king's negotiator in important discussions, and as ambassadors to other countries.
- ☑ Archbishop Lanfranc stood in for William when he went to Normandy, acting as his regent.

 How did the Normans change the Church in England ?

The Normans introduced important changes to the Church in England.

- ☑ Although many of the priests were still Anglo-Saxon, by 1070 William had replaced all of the important Anglo-Saxon churchmen with Normans.
- ☑ In 1070, the Anglo-Saxon Archbishop of Canterbury, Stigand, was replaced by Lanfranc.

 What did Lanfranc change about the Norman Church?

Archbishop Lanfranc made many reforms to the Church in England.

- ☑ He encouraged William to make the Archbishop of Canterbury the head of the Church in England, securing primacy over the Archbishop of York.
- ☑ He also changed several Church rituals.
- ☑ Lanfranc tightened up the restrictions on churchmen marrying or having sexual relationships.
- ☑ Lanfranc also set up Church courts in 1076 for churchmen who were accused of crimes. This gave the Church a lot of independence from the king, and an important role in the legal system.
- ☑ Anglo-Saxon churches were knocked down and rebuilt in the Norman (Romanesque) style, in key locations and market towns.
- ☑ Archdeacons - above priests but below bishops - became more and more common.
- ☑ Lanfranc, himself an Italian monk, encouraged the revival of monasteries and religious communities.

 Why did the Normans change the Norman Church?

William had gained the pope's support for his invasion in 1066 partly because he promised to reform the Church. There were a number of reasons why the Church needed reform.

- ☑ There were criticisms of pluralism - clergy holding more than one position, so that they could not effectively fulfil any one role.
- ☑ There were criticisms of nepotism - appointing family and friends to positions in the Church , rather than the best men for the job.
- ☑ There were criticisms of simony - when positions in the Church were sold to the highest bidder.
- ☑ There were also many instances of priests marrying and having children, even though this went against the rules of the Church.

Stigand, Archbishop of Canterbury, was a prime example of a corrupt priest. This was why William refused to be crowned by Stigand in 1066, because it might cause challenges to his legitimacy.

What was the Normanisation of the English Church in Norman England?

The Normans worked to put their stamp on the Church in England.

 By the 12th century, nearly every Anglo-Saxon church building (p.72) had been pulled down and replaced by new buildings in the Norman style.

Nearly every important Anglo-Saxon churchman had been replaced by a Norman.

How did the Norman Church help keep control for the Normans?

As well as representing Norman ideas, the Church became an effective tool for William to strengthen his hold over England.

Norman bishops and archbishops encouraged the preaching of positive messages about God's support of William and the Normans.

With Norman bishops and archbishops, Church land was effectively controlled by the Normans, which helped to prevent rebellions.

Lanfranc made sure that the Church had more control over priests, which meant that the Anglo-Saxons in the church were more effectively monitored by the Normans.

New bishops paid homage to the king.

The king approved Church Council decisions.

The king appointed new bishops, or replacements for those who died.

William controlled communication between the English Church and the pope.

DID YOU KNOW?

The Normans destroyed most Anglo-Saxon churches.

The Normans built larger stone churches - much like their big castles - and constructed huge basilicas in major towns, such as London, Durham and York, which could hold many hundreds of people. It was a display of power.

NORMAN CHURCH COURTS

The Church was even given its own law courts, which gave it immense power.

What were Church courts in Norman times?

Church courts were introduced by the Normans, and gave the Church the ability to try its own clergymen and to punish moral crimes. This gave the Church more legal powers.

How did Norman Church courts affect ordinary people?

William had encouraged the Church to set up Church courts to deal with moral crimes.

How did Norman Church courts affect churchmen?

The Church also claimed the right to try any churchman accused of a crime in its own courts, presided by the local bishop.

ROMANESQUE ARCHITECTURE

The Normans introduced a new style of architecture for castles and churches. This was known as Romanesque.

 What was Norman architecture like?

Norman architecture was often focused on creating the biggest, most imposing and impressive structures possible. New buildings, such as castles and cathedrals, were built in the Romanesque style, brought from the continent.

 How did their conquest of England affect Norman architecture?

One way in which the Normans emphasised their superiority over Anglo-Saxons was through the building of impressive new structures that were bigger and better than anything the Anglo-Saxons had.

- By the 12th century, every Anglo-Saxon cathedral and church had been demolished and rebuilt by the Normans in the Romanesque style.

- Norman buildings tended to be larger than any Anglo-Saxon buildings. Westminster Great Hall, for example, was the largest hall in Europe.

 What did Norman architecture look like?

The new Norman architecture was known as Romanesque. It used features that reminded people of the architecture of the Roman empire, hence its name.

- The overall impression was of size and grandeur. Romanesque buildings were much larger than anything the Saxons had been able to build.

- The Romanesque style was characterised by thick walls, round arches, sturdy pillars, and symmetry.

- Ceilings were vaulted, which allowed the interior to be much higher than in earlier buildings.

- Decorations seemed complex, but were made up of simple patterns such as chevrons and herring-bones.

DID YOU KNOW?

Romanesque castles and cathedrals

- ✓ Early stone-built castles employed Romanesque architecture. Examples include the Tower of London, Colchester Castle, and Rochester Castle.
- ✓ Durham Cathedral was one of earliest Romanesque cathedrals.
- ✓ Building cathedrals took such a long time that many incorporated later, Gothic features by the time they were completed.

RELATIONS WITH THE PAPACY

Because of the relationship between the king and the Church, the relationship of the king with the pope in Rome was crucial. It was not always a good relationship!

 What were relations like between kings and the pope?

The Norman kings' relationship with the pope was important, as it made a difference to their relationship with the Church in England. This relationship changed as time went on.

 What were King William I's relations with the pope like?

Saxon kings had not had close relations with the pope in Rome. William had a much closer relationship with the pope.

- Pope Alexander II had given William a papal banner in 1066, which gave his invasion God's blessing.
- Both William and Pope Alexander wanted to reform the Church in England, and bring it in line with European Christianity.
- Pope Gregory VII, however, wanted more papal control over the English Church, and this brought him into conflict with William.
- Pope Gregory wanted William to swear fealty to him, but William refused. He did not want the pope to interfere with his rights as king.
- However, William did agree to collect 'Peter's Pence', a special tax paid to the pope.

How did King William Rufus come into conflict with the Church?

There were 4 important reaons why William Rufus did not have a good relationship with the Church.

- Rufus was more interested in making money from the Church, and re-introduced simony. Ranulf Flambard paid £1,000 to become Bishop of Durham.
- Rufus also took land from the Church. He avoided appointing a new Archbishop of Canterbury in 1089, in order to profit from the lands that Lanfranc had held.
- The Church criticised Rufus' lifestyle. He might have been homosexual, which the Church disapproved of.
- Rufus challenged the power of the Church courts. He tried William of St-Calais, the Bishop of Durham, in a secular court, showing that he was determined to control the Church.

What were relations between King William Rufus and the pope like?

There were 6 important reasons why William Rufus came into conflict with the pope.

- When Rufus appointed Anselm as the new Archbishop of Canterbury in 1093, he refused to give back the Church lands he had taken over.
- By 1094, Anselm was preaching against Rufus, criticising his morals, and his behaviour towards the church.
- Rufus then prevented Anselm from travelling to Rome to receive the pallium. Rufus argued that this would mean he accepted the pope's influence over the English Church.
- In the end, Rufus reached an agreement with the pope. He accepted the pope's right to invest the new archbishop; the pope agreed to stay out of English affairs.
- Rufus and Anselm continued to argue, however, and Rufus blocked Anselm's attempts to make more reforms to the Church. Anselm also refused to pay additional taxes to the king.
- Finally, in 1097, Anselm was exiled, and he fled to Rome. Rufus took over his lands and continued to profit from them.

How did King Henry I come into conflict with the pope?

Henry I's (p.50) problems with the pope were to do with the 'Investiture Controversy'.

- Archbishop Anselm refused to perform homage to Henry, or to be invested by him. Henry exiled him in 1103.
- The pope threatened Henry with excommunication as a result.
- In 1107 they reached an agreement (the concordat of London).
- Henry agreed to give up his right to invest bishops. But he could still receive homage from them before they were invested.
- As a result, Henry could still treat bishops as his vassals, and they would have to provide knight (p.56) service if required.

What did the Investiture Controversy have to do with relations between king and pope?

The Investiture Controversy was an argument about who had more power - the king or the pope. It was a problem throughout Europe, not just in England.

- Kings expected to 'invest' bishops with the emblems of their office, and to receive homage from them.
- This was because bishops held land from the king, as tenants-in-chief.

☑ The Church opposed this, because it did not like the idea of churchmen paying homage to a secular ruler.

☑ If a tenant-in-chief *(p.56)* did not perform homage to the king, however, this would damage the king's authority in his own kingdom.

MONASTIC REFORM UNDER THE NORMANS

Monasteries were an important feature of medieval Christianity, and the Normans put a lot of effort into reforming monastic life.

 ### How did the Normans reform the monasteries?

As well as the reforms to the Church, the Normans made a number of reforms to monasteries in England.

 ### Why did the Normans reform the monasteries?

There were a number of reasons why the Normans wanted to reform the monasteries. These were problems that had been raised by the pope.

☑ Monasticism had declined in England. Many monasteries had been destroyed in Viking raids for two hundred years, and many of their treasures had been looted.

☑ Monasteries relied on gifts of land from secular lords. This raised the concern that monasteries had lost their independence.

☑ The was a great concern that monks were becoming lax, and were not following the Benedictine Rule properly.

 ### How did the Normans reform the monasteries?

After Lanfranc became Archbishop of Canterbury, he set about reforming the monasteries, at the same time that he was reforming the Church.

☑ Lanfranc reformed the liturgy (the words of church services), to make it more like that used in the rest of Europe.

☑ The role of the abbot was clearly defined, and a new monastic hierarchy was put in place.

☑ Lanfranc also created strict rules about when and how people could be made into saints.

☑ Lanfranc ensured that monks' lives were more strictly regulated. They would be seen to be more pious, and therefore they would be more respected.

☑ Over time, the Saxon leadership of the monasteries was replaced by Normans. In 1086, only three Saxon abbots remained in charge of monasteries.

 ### What were the Cluniac monasteries introduced by the Normans during the monastic reforms?

Cluniac monasteries were a new type of monastery, first introduced to England in 1077. They followed the Benedictine Rule, but were slightly different from other Benedictine monasteries.

☑ The Benedictine Rule was imposed more rigidly in Cluniac houses than at other monasteries.

☑ The Cluniac foundations were answerable only to the Abbot of Cluny in France. Therefore they were not subjected to secular interference.

☑ The leaders of Cluniac foundations had to travel to Cluny every year to meet with the Abbot. They dealt with any issues or problems together.

☑ Many Cluniac foundations were exempt from military service and other feudal duties. This meant that they were no subjected to secular interference.

 ### How successful were the Norman reforms to the monasteries?

The Norman reforms to monasticism were a success, and caused a great revival in monasticism in England.

- The number of monks and nuns in England increased. In 1066 there had been around 1,000, and by 1135 there were nearly 5,000.
- The number of monasteries grew, from around 60 to over 250.
- In 1066 there had been four cathedrals with attached monasteries. By 1135, ten out of 19 cathedrals had monasteries.
- The reforms were not accepted everywhere. At Glastonbury Abbey, in 1083, the monks refused to accept a new chant. The abbot sent knights to enforce the change, and three monks were killed, along with 18 wounded.

THE NORMAN LANGUAGE

The Normans even changed the use of language in England.

What language did the Normans speak?

The Normans spoke a form of French, known as Norman-French, which was an additional barrier between them and the English.

Could the Normans speak the English language?

With the Norman conquest, the language of the Anglo-Saxons became less important.

- English was only spoken by the common people, and only survived as a written language in a few places.
- William tried to learn *(p. 76)* English, but gave it up because he didn't have the time.
- Archbishop Lanfranc couldn't speak English.
- As time went on, more Normans learnt to speak both languages, and some Anglo-Saxons - such as Hereward the Wake - could speak French.

What was the official language in Norman England?

Under the Normans, English declined as the spoken language in certain areas, and it almost completely disappeared as a written language. Norman-French and Latin became the official languages.

- Norman French was the language of the king's court, and was the language used by the upper classes. It was also used for teaching.
- Over time, Norman-French developed into Anglo-Norman, as some English words were adopted.
- Under Norman rule, English disappeared from government and the Church. Latin became the language of government and the Church.
- Latin was also the language used by merchants who travelled overseas, as it was the language that all educated people in Europe spoke.

DID YOU KNOW?

It is estimated that around 46% of words in the English language are derived from Norman-French.

NORMAN EDUCATION

Education underwent a number of changes under Norman rule.

 ### Education in Norman England.

Almost all education was conducted by the Church and monasteries. It was not free, so most people had no access to education.

 ### What role did the Church play in Norman education?

The Church played an important role in Norman education.

- ✅ By 1100, all cathedrals had schools attached to them. Some had existed before the Norman Conquest.
- ✅ Some monasteries gave lessons to poor children, who 'paid' for their education by working as servants.
- ✅ Education did not become independent of the Church until the 14th Century, when a few secular schools were founded.

 ### What was Norman education like for girls?

Girls from noble families received some basic education, but girls were, in general, excluded from education.

 ### What subjects were taught in Norman education?

Education focused on the skills that boys needed for careers in the Church - Latin, music, astronomy and mathematics were the main subjects.

 ### Was university part of Norman education?

University education started under the Normans. Oxford University had started teaching by 1096. But Oxford was the only university in England until the foundation of Cambridge in 1209.

DID YOU KNOW?

There were some schools in Saxon England. King's School in Canterbury was founded in 597, and still educates young people today!

A

Abbot, Abbots - the male head of a monastery or leader of a group of monks.

Allegiance - loyalty to a person, group or cause.

Alliance - a union between groups or countries that benefits each member.

Allies - parties working together for a common objective, such as countries involved in a war. In both world wars, 'Allies' refers to those countries on the side of Great Britain.

Ambassador - someone, often a diplomat, who represents their state, country or organisation in a different setting or place.

Apothecaries, Apothecary - a non-medically trained person who concocted remedies from herbs.

Apprentice - an untrained person who works for a skilled employer, learning their trade.

Archbishop, Archbishops - a chief bishop in the Christian church, responsible for a major area.

Archer - someone who uses a bow and arrow; usually refers to those who used bows in warfare.

Aristocracy - the highest social class, whose members gain their power from possessing land, property and money.

Arson - the act of deliberately starting a fire.

Assassination - the act of murdering someone, usually an important person.

Autonomy - independence or self-government.

B

Barracks - a military building, or group of buildings, housing soldiers.

Bishop, Bishops - a senior member of the Christian Church, usually in charge of a diocese.

Blasphemy - the act of speaking insultingly about or with lack of reverence for God or sacred objects.

Boon work - the work a peasant did on his lord's land, usually for two or three days a week, often in lieu of paying rent for the peasant's own land.

Bribe, Bribery, Bribes - to dishonestly persuade someone to do something for you in return for money or other inducements.

C

Campaign - a political movement to get something changed; in military terms, it refers to a series of operations to achieve a goal.

Cathedral, Cathedrals - the principal church in a diocese, with which a bishop is associated.

Cavalry - the name given to soldiers who fight on horseback.

Ceorl - a peasant who was free to leave their lord's land to seek work elsewhere, sometimes known as a freeman.

Charter - a legal written grant, issued by a monarch or country's legislative power, permitting certain rights or privileges.

Claim - someone's assertion of their right to something - for example, a claim to the throne.

Clergy - those ordained for religious duties, especially in the Christian Church.

Collective responsibility - when a group of people is held responsible for an action or outcome, regardless of anyone's individual behaviour or performance.

Commissions - the collective term for several organisations set up by the League of Nations to solve global issues.

Consolidate - to strengthen a position, often politically, by bringing several things together into a more effective whole.

Coronation - the ceremony of crowning a monarch.

Corrupt - when someone is willing to act dishonestly for their own personal gain.

Counterfeit - a fake or fraudulent imitation, intended to deceive someone into believing it is genuine.

Currency - an umbrella term for any form of legal tender, but most commonly referring to money.

D

Demesne - land owned and retained under the direct control of a lord rather than leased out to a sub-tenant.

Deploy - to move military troops or equipment into position or a place so they are ready for action.

Destrier - a Norman war horse, bred and trained to be strong and vicious in battle.

Deterrent - something that discourages an action or behaviour.

Dispute - a disagreement or argument; often used to describe conflict between different countries.

E

Earl, Earls - the most important men in the country after the monarch during medieval times.

Earldom - area of land governed by an earl or high-ranking noble.

Economic - relating to the economy; also used when justifying something in terms of profitability.

Economy - a country, state or region's position in terms of production and consumption of goods and services, and the supply of money.

Embassy - historically, a deputation sent by one ruler, state or country to another. More recently, it is also the accepted name for the official residence or offices of an ambassador.

Empire - a group of states or countries ruled over and controlled by a single monarch.

Estate, Estates - an extensive area of land, usually in the country and including a large house. It tends to be owned by one person, family or organisation.

Excommunicate, Excommunication - to formally expel someone from the Catholic Church. Someone who is excommunicated is forbidden from participating in sacraments and services, and often believes their soul is condemned.

Exile - to be banned from one's original country, usually as a punishment or for political reasons.

F

Famine - a severe food shortage resulting in starvation and death, usually the result of bad harvests.

Fealty - another word for loyalty.

Feudal - relating to the feudal system.

Fief - an area or estate held by a vassal as part of the feudal system in medieval England.

Frontier - a line or border between two areas.

Fyrd - an army that could be raised by the king if needed to fight in Anglo-Saxon England. Every five hides had to provide a man to fight in the fyrd for a maximum of 40 days.

G

Guerrilla tactics, Guerrilla warfare - a way of fighting that typically involves hit-and-run style tactics.

Guerrillas - groups of small, independent fighters usually involved in a war against larger, regular military forces.

Guild, Guild system - organised groups that controlled different jobs, including apprenticeships and licensing for their specific profession.

H

Harvest - the process of gathering and collecting crops.

Heir - someone who is entitled to property or rank following the current owner or holder's death.

Hide - a measurement of land in Saxon times, equivalent to around 120 acres.

Hierarchies, Hierarchy - the ranking of people according to authority, for example a colonel in the army being higher than a corporal.

Homage - to demonstrate allegiance or respect to another in public.

I

Illegitimate - the term given to a child born to unmarried parents; generally, not authorised by law.

Independence, Independent - to be free of control, often meaning by another country, allowing the people of a nation the ability to govern themselves.

Infantry - soldiers who march and fight on foot.

Interpretation, Interpretations - a perceived meaning or particular explanation of something.

J

Journeyman - someone who has finished an apprenticeship, considered to have skill and experience, but who is not yet a master with his own business.

L

Lease, Leases - a contract granting the use of something such as land or property for a specified period of time, usually in return for payment.

Legitimacy, Legitimate - accepted by law or conforming to the rules; can be defended as valid.

Literate - someone who can read and write.

Lord, Lords - a man of high status, wealth and authority.

M

Mass - an act of worship in the Catholic Church.

Mercenary - someone who takes action in order to earn money, rather than out of principle.

Merchant, Merchants - someone who sells goods or services.

Military force - the use of armed forces.

Militia - an army created from the general population.

Monasteries, Monastery - a religious building occupied by monks

Monastic - relating to monks or others living under religious vows, or to the building they live in.

Monk - a member of a religious community, often living a simple life of poverty, chastity and work.

Morale - general mood of a group of people.

Morals - a person's set of rules about what they consider right and wrong, used to guide their actions and behaviour.

N

Nepotism - the practice of people in power favouring friends and family, often by giving them jobs or influence. Historically, this was especially common in government and the Church.

Nobility - the social class ranked directly below royalty.

Noble, Nobles - another word for aristocrat - a member of the highest and richest class in society.

O

Oath - a solemn promise with special significance, often relating to future behaviour or actions.

P

Pallium - part of the ecclesiastical vestments, comprising bands that hang in front of the robes and down the back. It is given to archbishops and bishops as confirmation of their appointment.

Papal - relating to the pope.

Peasant - a poor farmer.

Penance - a punishment willingly undertaken or inflicted on oneself to show sorrow and repentance for committing a sin, and to gain forgiveness.

Pious - devoutly religious.

Pluralism - the practice, especially in the church, of holding more than one job at a time. There was concern that a person could not do any job properly because their attention was divided.

Pope - the head of the Roman Catholic Church.

Population - the number of people who live in a specified place.

Pragmatic - taking a practical approach; being sensible and realistic.

Preach, Preaching - to deliver a religious speech or sermon to a group of people.

Predecessor - the person who came before; the previous person to fill a role or position.

Prevent, Preventative, Preventive - steps taken to stop something from happening.

Proclamation - a public or official announcement of great importance.

Profit - generally refers to financial gain; the amount of money made after deducting buying, operating or production costs.

R

Raid - a quick surprise attack on the enemy.

Rallies, Rally - a political event with speakers and a crowd, designed to increase support for a politician, political party or an idea.

Rebellion - armed resistance against a government or leader, or resistance to other authority or control.

Rebels - people who rise in opposition or armed resistance against an established government or leader.

Reform, Reforming - change, usually in order to improve an institution or practice.

Refugee, Refugees - a person who has been forced to leave where they live due to war, disaster or persecution.

Regent - the person who rules when the king is away, incapacitated or too young to rule.

Reign - a period of power, usually by a monarch.

Repent, Repented, Repenting - to feel or express remorse and regret for one's wrongdoings or sins.

Romanesque - a style of architecture from the final period of the Roman Empire.

S

Secular - unconnected to religious or spiritual matters; not bound by religious rule.

Sheriff, Sheriffs - an important royal official in medieval England, responsible for running the local court and ensuring tax was paid to the monarch.

Shield wall - a highly effective battle tactic where soldiers would stand in a row with their shields overlapping.

Shire - a defined area of land in England during the Saxon and medieval periods, later known as a county.

Simony - the practice, especially in the church, of selling offices or roles rather than appointing people on their merits.

Sin - in religion, an immoral act against God's laws.

Strategy - a plan of action outlining how a goal will be achieved.

Submission, Submit - a formal surrender and acceptance of a new authority.

Successor - someone who succeeds the previous person, such as a leader who takes over the role from the previous holder.

T

Tactic - a strategy or method of achieving a goal.

Tenant-In-chief, Tenants-In-chief - a person who controlled land leased to them by the monarch.

Territories, Territory - an area of land under the control of a ruler/country.

The crown, The throne - phrases used to represent royal power. For example, if someone 'seizes the throne' it means they have taken control. Can also refer to physical objects.

Thegn - the local lord in Anglo-Saxon times, a wealthy and important man. Thegns owned more than 5 hides of land and rented it out to peasants.

Treason - the crime of betraying one's country, often involving an attempt to overthrow the government or kill the monarch.

Treasury - a place or building where money or treasure is held; also refers to a government department related to finance and taxation.

U

Upper class - a socio-economic group consisting of the richest people in a society who are wealthy because they own land or property.

V

Vassal - someone who held their land in return for service and was expected to swear oaths of homage and fealty to their lord.

Villein - an unfree peasant, tied to the land where he lived and unable to leave without his lord's permission.

Wergild - meaning 'man price', this was the value placed on a man's life in Saxon England and the amount of compensation to be paid for his injury or death.

Writ - a written command from a court or other legal authority.

Quizzes, amazing exam preparation tools and more at GCSEHistory.com

Lightning Source UK Ltd.
Milton Keynes UK
UKHW050802120822
407197UK00003B/60